EYEWITNESS TRAVEL GUIDES

ITALIAN
PHRASE BOOK

D1418990

A Dorling Kindersley Book

LONDON, NEW YORK, MUNICH,
MELBOURNE, AND DELHI

Compiled by Lexus Ltd with Karen McAulay and Mariarosaria Cardines
Printed and bound in Italy by Printer Trento Srl.

First published in Great Britain in 1997
by Dorling Kindersley Limited
80 Strand, London WC2R ORL

Reprinted with corrections 2000, 2002
6 8 10 9 7 5

Dorling Kindersley books can be purchased in bulk quantities at
discounted prices for use in promotions or as premiums. We are
also able to offer special editions and personalized jackets, corporate
imprints, and excerpts from all of our books, tailored specifically to
meet your own needs. To find out more, please contact: Special Sales,
Dorling Kindersley Limited, 80 Strand, London WC2R ORL;
Tel. 020 7753 3572.

A CIP catalogue record is available from the British Library.

ISBN 0 7513 6987 X

See our complete catalogue at
www.dk.com

CONTENTS

PREFACE

This *Dorling Kindersley Eyewitness Travel Guides Phrase Book* has been compiled by experts to meet the general needs of tourists and business travellers. Arranged under headings such as Hotels, Driving and so forth, the ample selection of useful words and phrases is supported by a 2,000-line mini-dictionary. There is also an extensive menu guide listing approximately 600 dishes or methods of cooking and presentation.

Typical replies to questions you may ask during your journey, and the signs or instructions you may see or hear, are shown in tinted boxes. In the main text, the pronunciation of Italian words and phrases is imitated in English sound syllables. The Introduction provides guidelines to Italian pronunciation.

Dorling Kindersley Eyewitness Travel Guides are recognized as the world's best travel guides. Each title features specially commissioned colour photographs, detailed maps, cutaways of major buildings and 3-D aerial views, plus information on sights, events, hotels, restaurants, shopping and entertainment.

Dorling Kindersley Eyewitness Travel Guides titles include:
Italy · Florence & Tuscany · Milan & the Lakes · Naples
Rome · Sardinia · Sicily · Venice & the Veneto · Amsterdam
Australia · Sydney · Berlin · Budapest · California · Florida
Hawaii · New York · San Francisco & Northern California · Canada
France · Loire Valley · Paris · Provence · Great Britain · London
Ireland · Dublin · Scotland · Greece: Athens & the Mainland
The Greek Islands · Istanbul · Jerusalem & the Holy Land · Mexico
Moscow · St Petersburg · Portugal · Lisbon · Prague
South Africa · Spain · Barcelona · Madrid · Seville & Andalusia
Thailand · Vienna · Warsaw

INTRODUCTION

PRONUNCIATION

The pronunciation of an Italian word is very similar to the way it is written. When reading the imitated pronunciation, stress the part that is underlined. Pronounce each syllable as if it formed part of an English word and you will be understood. Remember the points below, and your pronunciation will be even closer to the correct Italian.

ai	as in 'fair'
ay	as in 'pay'
e	as in 'bed'
	(pronounced as a separate syllable at the end of a word)
g	always hard as in 'get'
I	as in 'I'
ow	as in 'cow'
r	always strongly pronounced
y	always pronounced as in 'yet,' except in *ay* as above

Note that when there are two identical consonants separated by a hyphen, eg **vorrei** – *vor-ray*, both consonants must be pronounced as if you were pronouncing two separate English words: eg 'jus<u>t t</u>wo', 'fu<u>ll l</u>ength'.

GENDERS AND ARTICLES

Italian has two genders for nouns – masculine and feminine. In the vocabulary section of this book, we generally give the definite article ('the'). For masculine nouns, the definite article is **il** (plural **i**) before nouns beginning with a consonant, **lo** (plural **gli**) before nouns beginning with 's' + consonant or with 'z', and **l'** (plural **gli**) before nouns beginning with a vowel. For feminine nouns, use **la** before a noun beginning with a consonant and **l'** before a vowel (plural **le**).

The masculine indefinite article ('a') is **uno** before a noun beginning with a consonant and **un** before a vowel. The feminine is **una** before a consonant and **un'** before a vowel.

USEFUL EVERYDAY PHRASES

Yes, No, OK, etc.

Yes/No
Sì/No
see/no

Excellent!
Ottimo!
ot-teemo

Don't!
Non farlo!
non farlo

OK
OK
'ok'

That's fine
Va bene
va bene

That's right
È vero
eh vayro

Greetings, Introductions

How do you do, pleased to meet you
Piacere di conoscerla
pee-achaire dee konoshairla

Good morning/Good evening/Good night
Buon giorno/Buona sera/Buona notte
bwon jorno/bwona saira/bwona not-te

Goodbye
Arrivederci
ar-reevedairchee

How are you?　　　　　　　*(familiar)*
Come sta?　　　　　　　　　Come stai?
kome sta　　　　　　　　　*kome stı*

My name is …
Mi chiamo …
mee k-yamo

What's your name?　　　　*(familiar)*
Come si chiama?　　　　　　Come ti chiami?
kome see k-yama　　　　　*kome tee k-yamee*

What's his/her name?
Come si chiama?
kome see k-yama

May I introduce …?
Posso presentarle …?
pos-so prezentarle

This is … *(introducing male/female)*
Questo è …/Questa è …
kwesto eh/kwesta eh

Hello/Hi!
Ciao/Salve!
chow/salve

Bye!
Ciao!
chow

See you later
A più tardi
a p-yoo tardee

It's been nice meeting you
Mi ha fatto piacere conoscerla
mee a fat-to pee-achaire konoshairla

PLEASE, THANK YOU, APOLOGIES

Thank you/No, thank you
Grazie/No grazie
gratzee-e/no gratzee-e

Yes, please
Sì, grazie
see gratzee-e

Please *(offering)*   *(asking for something)*
Prego   Per favore/per piacere
prego   *pair favore/pair pee-achaire*

Excuse me! *(when burping, sneezing, etc)*
Scusate!
skoozate

Sorry!   *(familiar)*
Scusi!   Scusa!
skoozee   *skooza*

I'm really sorry
Sono davvero spiacente
sono dav-vairo spee-achente

It was/wasn't my fault!
È stato/non è stata colpa mia!
eh stato/non eh stata kolpa mee-a

WHERE, HOW, ASKING

Excuse me, please *(to get past etc)*
Permesso
pairmesso

Can you tell me …?
Potrebbe dirmi …?
potreb-be deermee

Can I have …?
Potrei avere …?
potray avaire

Would you like a …?
Vorrebbe un/una …?
vor-reb-be oon/oona

Would you like to …?
Le piacerebbe …?
le pee-achaireb-be

Is there … here?
C'è …?
cheh

What's that?
Che cos'è?
ke kozeh

Where can I get …?
Dove potrei trovare …?
dove potray trovare

How much is it?
Quanto costa?
kwanto kosta

Where is the …?
Dov'è il/la …?
doveh eel/la

Where are the toilets, please?
Per cortesia, dove sono i gabinetti?
pair kortezee-a dove sono ee gabee-net-tee

USEFUL EVERYDAY PHRASES

Is there wheelchair access?
È possibile l'accesso con la sedia a rotelle?
eh pos-see-bee-leh l'aches-so kon la saidee-a rotail-le

Are there facilities for the disabled?
Ci sono facilità per gli handicappati?
chee sono fachee-lee-ta pair l-yee andee-kap-patee

Are guide dogs allowed?
È permesso portare i cani guida?
eh pairmes-so portarai ee kanee gweeda

ABOUT ONESELF

I'm from …
Sono di …
sono dee

I'm … years old
Ho … anni
o … an-nee

I'm a … *(occupation)*
Faccio il/la …
facho eel/la

I'm married/single/divorced *(said by a man)*
Sono sposato/celibe/divorziato
sono spozato/cheleebe/deevortz-yato

(said by a woman)
Sono sposata/nubile/divorziata
sono spozata/noobeele/deevortz-yata

I have … sisters/brothers/children
Ho … sorelle/fratelli/bambini
o … sorel-le/fratel-lee/bambeenee

LIKES, DISLIKES, SOCIALIZING

I like/love …
Mi piace …
mee pee-ache

I don't like …
Non mi piace …
non mee pee-ache

I like swimming/travelling
Mi piace nuotare/viaggiare
mee pee-ache nwotare/vyaj-jare

I hate …
Odio …
odee-o

Do you like …?
Le piace …?
le pee-ache

It's delicious/awful!
È buonissimo/terribile!
eh bwonees-seemo/ter-reebeele

I don't drink/smoke
Non bevo/fumo
non bevo/foomo

Do you mind if I smoke?
Le dispiace se fumo?
le deespee-ache se foomo

I don't eat meat or fish
Non mangio nè la carne nè il pesce
non manjo neh la karne neh eel peshe

What would you like (to drink)?
Cosa desidera (da bere)?
koza dezeedaira da baire

I would like a …
Vorrei un/una …
vor-re oon/oona

Nothing for me, thanks
Per me niente, grazie
pair me nee-ente gratzee-e

I'll get this one
Prenderò questo
prendairo kwesto

Cheers! *(toast)*
Alla salute!/Cin cin!
al-la saloote/cheen cheen

I would like to …
Vorrei …
vor-ray

Let's go to Florence/the cinema/the exhibition
Andiamo a Firenze/al cinema/alla mostra
and-yamo a feerentze/al cheenema/al-la mostra

Let's go swimming/for a walk
Andiamo a nuotare/a fare una passeggiata
and-yamo a nwotare/a fare oona pas-sej-jata

What's the weather like?
Che tempo fa?
ke tempo fa

The weather's awful
È brutto tempo
eh broot-to tempo

It's pouring down
Sta piovendo a dirotto
sta p-yovendo a deerot-to

It's really hot
Fa veramente caldo
fa veramente kaldo

It's sunny
C'è il sole
cheh eel sole

HELP, PROBLEMS

Can you help me?
Può aiutarmi?
pwo I-ootarmee

I don't understand
Non capisco
non kapeesko

Do you speak English/French/German?
Parla inglese/francese/tedesco?
parla eengleze/francheze/tedesko

Does anyone here speak English?
C'è qualcuno che parla inglese?
cheh kwalkoono ke parla eengleze

I can't speak Italian
Non parlo italiano
non parlo eetal-yano

I don't know
Non so
non so

What's wrong?
Cosa c'è che non va?
koza cheh ke non va

Please speak more slowly
Per favore, parli più lentamente
pair favore parlee p-yoo lentamente

Please write it down for me
Me lo scriva, per favore
me lo skreeva pair favore

I'm lost *(said by a man/woman)*
Mi sono perso/persa
mee sono pairso/pairsa

Go away! *(familiar)*
Se ne vada!   Vattene!
se ne vada   *vat-tene*

TALKING TO RECEPTIONISTS ETC

I have an appointment with …
Ho un appuntamento con …
o oon ap-poontamento kon

I'd like to see …
Vorrei vedere …
vor-ray vedaire

Here's my card
Questo è il mio biglietto da visita
kwesto eh eel mee-o beel-yet-to da veez-eeta

My company is …
La mia società è …
la mee-a socheta eh

May I use your phone?
Posso usare il telefono?
pos-so oozare eel telefono

THINGS YOU'LL SEE

acqua potabile	drinking water
affittasi	to let
aperto	open
ascensore	lift
buffet	snack bar
cassa	till, cash point
chiuso	closed
chiuso per ferie	closed for holiday period
entrata	entrance
entrata libera	free admission
feriali	working days
festivi	public holidays
gabinetti	toilets
libero	vacant, free
occupato	engaged
orario di apertura	opening hours
orario di visita	visiting hours
piano terra	ground floor
primo piano	first floor
riservato	reserved
saldi/sconti	sales
servizi	toilets
signore	women
signori	men
si prega di non ...	please do not ...
spingere	push
strada	road
svendita	sale
tirare	pull
ufficio informazioni	tourist information
uscita	exit
uscita di sicurezza	emergency exit
vendesi	for sale
vernice fresca	wet paint

→

via	street
vietato	forbidden
vietato l'ingresso	no admittance

THINGS YOU'LL HEAR

a più tardi	see you later
arrivederci	goodbye
attenzione!	look out! pay attention!
avanti!	come in!
bene	good, fine
buon viaggio!	have a good trip!
come stai/sta/state?	how are you?
come va?	how are things?
cosa hai/ha detto?	what did you say?
davvero?	really?
ecco-ti qua!	here you are!
esattamente	exactly
grazie	thanks
grazie, anche a lei	thank you, the same to you
mi dispiace tanto!	I'm so sorry!
mi scusi	excuse me
molte grazie	thank you very much
molto bene, grazie	very well, thank you
– e lei?	– and you?
non capisco	I don't understand
non so	I don't know
prego	you're welcome, don't mention it
prego?	pardon?
serviti/si serva/servitevi	help yourself
scusi?, come?	excuse me?
sì	yes
va bene	that's right

COLLOQUIALISMS

You may hear these. To use some of them yourself could be risky!

accidenti!	damn!
che schifo!	it's disgusting!
chiudi il becco!	shut up!
cretino	idiot, fool
Dio mio!	my God!
e allora?	so what?
è orribile!	it's awful!
fa' pure!	do as you please; please, do!
grazie a Dio!	thank God!
maledetto …	cursed …
maledizione!	damn!
ma va?	really?
ma va!	I don't believe it
meglio così	so much the better
muoviti!	hurry up!
non posso crederci!	I can't believe it!
occhio!	watch out!
per Dio!	by God!
porca miseria!	oh, hell!
prova!	just try!
sei pazzo?	you must be crazy!
sparisci!	scram!
stupendo!	great!
svitato	crazy, nuts
ti sta bene!	it serves you right!
tizio	bloke
togliti dai piedi!	get out of the way!
va al diavolo!/va all'inferno!	go to hell!
va a quel paese!	get lost!
va bene!	that's fine; it's OK!
zitto!	shut up!

DAYS, MONTHS, SEASONS

Sunday	domenica	*domeneeka*
Monday	lunedì	*loonedee*
Tuesday	martedì	*martedee*
Wednesday	mercoledì	*mairkoledee*
Thursday	giovedì	*jovedee*
Friday	venerdì	*venairdee*
Saturday	sabato	*sabato*
January	gennaio	*jen-na-yo*
February	febbraio	*feb-bra-yo*
March	marzo	*martzo*
April	aprile	*apreele*
May	maggio	*maj-jo*
June	giugno	*joon-yo*
July	luglio	*lool-yo*
August	agosto	*agosto*
September	settembre	*set-tembre*
October	ottobre	*ot-tobre*
November	novembre	*novembre*
December	dicembre	*deechembre*
Spring	primavera	*preemavaira*
Summer	estate	*estate*
Autumn	autunno	*owtoon-no*
Winter	inverno	*eenvairno*
Christmas	Natale	*natale*
Christmas Eve	la Vigilia di Natale	*veejeel-ya dee natale*
Good Friday	Venerdì Santo	*venairdee santo*
Easter	Pasqua	*paskwa*
New Year	Capodanno	*kapodan-no*
New Year's Eve	San Silvestro	*san seelvestro*
Pentecost	Pentecoste	*pentekoste*

NUMBERS

0	zero *tzairo*	10	dieci *dee-echee*
1	uno *oono*	11	undici *oon-deechee*
2	due *doo-e*	12	dodici *doh-deechee*
3	tre *tre*	13	tredici *tre-deechee*
4	quattro *kwat-tro*	14	quattordici *kwat-tor-deechee*
5	cinque *cheenkwe*	15	quindici *kween-deechee*
6	sei *say*	16	sedici *say-deechee*
7	sette *set-te*	17	diciassette *deechas-set-te*
8	otto *ot-to*	18	diciotto *deechot-to*
9	nove *no-ve*	19	diciannove *deechan-no-ve*

20	venti	*ventee*
21	ventuno	*vent-oono*
22	ventidue	*ventee-doo-e*
30	trenta	*trenta*
31	trentuno	*trentoono*
32	trentadue	*trentadoo-e*
40	quaranta	*kwaranta*
50	cinquanta	*cheenkwanta*
60	sessanta	*ses-santa*
70	settanta	*set-tanta*
80	ottanta	*ot-tanta*
90	novanta	*novanta*
100	cento	*chento*
110	centodieci	*chento-dee-echee*
200	duecento	*doo-e-chento*
1,000	mille	*meele*
10,000	diecimila	*dee-echeemeela*
20,000	ventimila	*venteemeela*
50,000	cinquantamila	*cheenkwantameela*
54,250	cinquantaquattromila duecentocinquanta	*cheenkwanta-kwat-tro-meela doo-e-chento-cheenkwanta*
100,000	centomila	*chentomeela*
1,000,000	un milione	*oon meel-yone*

Note that thousands are written 1.000, 10.000, etc, in Italian.

TIME

today	oggi	*oj-jee*
yesterday	ieri	*yairee*
tomorrow	domani	*domanee*
the day before yesterday	l'altro ieri	*laltro yairee*
the day after tomorrow	dopodomani	*dopodomanee*
this week	questa settimana	*kwesta set-teemana*
last week	la settimana scorsa	*set-teemana skorsa*
next week	la settimana prossima	*set-teemana pros-seema*
this morning	stamattina	*stamat-teena*
this afternoon	questo pomeriggio	*kwesto pomereej-jo*
this evening	stasera	*stasaira*
tonight	stanotte	*stanot-te*
yesterday afternoon	ieri pomeriggio	*yairee pomereej-jo*
last night	ieri sera, ieri notte	*yairee saira, yairee not-te*
tomorrow morning	domani mattina	*domanee mat-teena*
tomorrow night	domani sera	*domanee saira*
in three days	tra tre giorni	*tra tre jornee*
three days ago	tre giorni fa	*tre jornee fa*
late	tardi	*tardee*
early	presto	*presto*
soon	presto	*presto*
later on	più tardi	*p-yoo tardee*
at the moment	in questo momento	*een kwesto momento*
second	un secondo	*sekondo*
minute	un minuto	*meenooto*
two minutes	due minuti	*doo-e meenootee*
quarter of an hour	un quarto d'ora	*kwarto dora*
half an hour	mezz'ora	*medzora*
three quarters of an hour	tre quarti d'ora	*tre kwartee dora*

20

hour	un'ora	_ora_
day	un giorno	_jorno_
week	una settimana	_set-teemana_
fortnight	quindici giorni	_kween-deechee jornee_
month	un mese	_meze_
year	un anno	_an-no_
that day	quel giorno	_kwel jorno_
every day	ogni giorno	_on-yee jorno_
all day	tutto il giorno	_toot-to eel jorno_
the next day	il giorno dopo	_jorno dopo_

TELLING THE TIME

The hour is expressed in Italian by the ordinal number only: **sono le due** 'it's two o'clock', **alle due** 'at two o'clock'. There is no equivalent of 'o'clock'. To denote the half hour, add **e mezza** after the hour: **sono le due e mezza** 'it's 2.30'. To say 'quarter past', add **e un quarto** 'and a quarter' to the hour: **sono le tre e un quarto** is 'it's a quarter past three'.

Quarter to the hour is expressed either by adding **e tre quarti** 'and three quarters' to the hour, or adding **meno un quarto** 'less a quarter' to the next hour. 'It's a quarter to eight' is therefore **sono le sette e tre quarti** _or_ **sono le otto meno un quarto**.

To express minutes after the hour, add the minutes to the hour: **sono le sette e quaranta** 'it's seven forty'. Minutes to the hour are expressed by adding **meno** followed by the number of minutes to the next hour: **sono le otto meno venti** 'it's twenty to eight'.

There are no equivalents of am and pm in Italian, although you could use **di mattina/del mattino** 'in the morning,' **di/del pomeriggio** 'in the afternoon,' **di sera** 'in the evening,' and **di notte** 'at night'. For example: '10 am' is **le dieci di mattina/del mattino**; '6 pm' is **le sei di/del pomeriggio**; '10 pm' is **le dieci di sera**; '2 am' is **le due di notte** (but also **le due del mattino**).

The 24-hour clock is also used, both in the written form as in timetables, and verbally as in enquiry offices and when making appointments.

what time is it?	che ore sono?	*ke ore sono?*
it's one o'clock	è l'una	*eh loona*
it's two/three/four o'clock	sono le due/tre/quattro	*sono le doo-e/tre/kwat-tro*
ten past one	l'una e dieci	*loona ay dee-echee*
quarter past one	l'una e un quarto	*loona ay oon kwarto*
1.30	l'una e mezza	*loona ay medza*
twenty to two	le due meno venti	*lay doo-e meno ventee*
quarter to two	le due meno un quarto	*le doo-e meno oon kwarto*
two o'clock	le due	*le doo-e*
13.00	le tredici	*le tre-deechee*
16.30	le sedici e trenta	*le se-deechee ay trenta*
at 5.30	alle cinque e mezza	*al-le cheenkwe ay medza*
at seven o'clock	alle sette	*al-le set-te*
noon	mezzogiorno	*medzojorno*
midnight	mezzanotte	*medzanot-te*

THE CALENDAR

The cardinal numbers on page 19 are used to express the date in Italian, except for the first when the ordinal **il primo** is used:

the first of May	il primo maggio	*eel preemo maj-jo*
the second of September	il due settembre	*eel doo-e set-tembre*
the twentieth of June	il venti giugno	*eel ventee joon-yo*

HOTELS

Hotels in Italy are classified according to the familiar star system: one, two, three, four and five stars. At the bottom of the range you'll find **locande** (one-star hotels) and **pensioni** (one- or two-star hotels). The prices are displayed in the rooms and they do not always include breakfast, but should include service charges and taxes.

In some areas, the local **APT** (**Azienda di Promozione Turistica**) can supply information about hotels, but in others tourism is coordinated by an **AAST** (**Azienda Autonoma di Soggiorno e Turismo**). It is also possible to obtain a list of hotels from information offices in stations and airports. If you arrive in a town without having reserved beforehand, go directly to the **APT** or to the **AAST** for help. Leaflets will be available in English, and usually at least one person there will speak English.

Hotel breakfasts mainly consist of a **brioche** (a type of croissant) or bread, butter and jam, and coffee or tea. Some hotels may provide a full breakfast on request.

USEFUL WORDS AND PHRASES

balcony	il balcone	*bal-kone*
bath	la vasca da bagno	*vaska da ban-yo*
bathroom	il bagno	*ban-yo*
bed	il letto	*let-to*
bed and breakfast	camera con colazione	*kamaira kon kolatz-yone*
bed and breakfast hotel	la pensione familiare	*penz-yone fameel-yare*
bedroom	la camera da letto	*kamaira da let-to*
bill	il conto	*konto*
breakfast	la prima colazione	*preema kolatz-yone*
dining room	la sala da pranzo	*sala da prantzo*
dinner	la cena	*chena*

double bed	il letto matrimoniale	_let-to matreemonyale_
double room	la stanza doppia	_stantza doppee-a_
lift	l'ascensore	_ashen-sore_
foyer	la hall	_oll_
full board	la pensione	_pens-yone_
	completa	_kompleta_
guesthouse	la pensione,	_pens-yone,_
	la locanda	_lokanda_
half board	la mezza pensione	_medza pens-yone,_
hotel	l'albergo, l'hotel	_albairgo, oh-tel_
key	la chiave	_k-yave_
lounge	il salone	_salone_
lunch	il pranzo,	_prantzo,_
	la seconda colazione	_sekonda kolatz-yone_
maid	la cameriera	_kamair-yaira_
manager	il direttore	_deeret-tore_
car park	il parcheggio	_parkej-jo_
receipt	la ricevuta	_reechevoota_
reception	la reception	_'reception'_
receptionist	il/la receptionist	_'receptionist'_
restaurant	il ristorante	_reestorante_
room	la camera, la stanza	_kamaira, stantza_
room service	il servizio in camera	_serveetz-yo een_
		kamaira
shower	la doccia	_docha_
single bed	il letto singolo	_let-to seengolo_
single room	la stanza singola	_stantza seengola_
sink	il lavandino	_lavandeeno_
toilet	la toilette	_twalet_
twin room	la stanza con due	_stantza kon doo-e_
	letti	_lettee_

Have you any vacancies?
Avete una stanza libera?
avete oona stantza leebaira

I have a reservation
Ho prenotato una stanza
o prenotato oona stantza

I'd like a single room
Vorrei una stanza singola
vor-ray oona stantza seengola

I'd like a room with a bathroom/balcony
Vorrei una stanza con bagno/con il balcone
vor-ray oona stantza kon ban-yo/kon eel bal-kone

Is there satellite/cable TV in the rooms?
C'è la TV satellite/cavo in queste stanze?
Cheh la tee-vee satail-lee-te/kavo een kwaiste stantze

I'd like a room for one night/three nights
Vorrei una stanza per una notte/tre notti
vor-ray oona stantza pair oona not-te/tre not-tee

What is the charge per night?
Quanto si paga per notte?
kwanto see paga pair not-te

I don't know yet how long I'll stay
Non so ancora quanto tempo rimarrò
non so ankora kwanto tempo reemarro

When is breakfast/dinner?
A che ora viene servita la colazione/la cena?
a ke ora v-yene serveeta la kolatz-yone/la chena

Please wake me at ... o'clock
Mi svegli, per favore, alle ...
mee zvel-yee pair favore al-le

Can I have breakfast in my room?
Potrei avere la colazione in camera?
potray avaire la kolatz-yone een kamaira

I'd like to have some laundry done
Vorrei far pulire alcuni indumenti
vor-ray far pooleere alkoonee eendoomentee

I'll be back at … o'clock
Tornerò alle …
tornairo al-le

My room number is …
Il mio numero di stanza è …
eel mee-o noomero dee stantza eh …

My booking was for a double room
Avevo prenotato una stanza doppia
avevo prenotato oona stantza dop-pia

I asked for a room with a en suite bathroom
Avevo chiesto una stanza con bagno
avevo k-yesto oona stantza kon ban-yo

There is no toilet paper in the bathroom
Non c'è carta igienica in bagno
non cheh karta eej-yeneeka een ban-yo

The window won't open
La finestra non si apre
la feenestra non see apre

The lift/shower isn't working
L'ascensore/la doccia non funziona
lashen-sore/la docha non foontz-yona

There isn't any hot water
Non c'è acqua calda
non cheh akwa kalda

The socket in the bathroom doesn't work
La presa di corrente del bagno non funziona
la preza dee kor-rente del ban-yo non foontz-yona

I'm leaving tomorrow
Parto domani
parto domanee

When do I have to vacate the room?
Entro che ora devo liberare la camera?
entro ke ora devo leebairare la kamaira

Can I have the bill, please?
Mi da il conto, per favore?
mee da eel konto pair favore

I'll pay by credit card
Pago con la carta di credito
pago kon la karta dee kredeeto

I'll pay cash
Pago in contanti
pago een kontantee

Can you get me a taxi, please?
Potrebbe chiamarmi un taxi, per favore?
potreb-be k-yamarmee oon 'taxi' pair favore

Can you recommend another hotel?
Potrebbe consigliarmi un altro albergo?
potreb-be konseel-yarmee oon altro albairgo

THINGS YOU'LL SEE

albergo	hotel
ascensore	lift
bagno	bathroom
camera con prima colazione	bed and breakfast
cena	dinner
chiave	key
colazione	breakfast
completo	no vacancies

→

conto	bill
entrata	entrance
locanda	guesthouse
mezza pensione	half board
parcheggio	car park
parcheggio riservato agli ospiti dell'albergo	parking reserved for hotel patrons only
pensione	guesthouse
pensione completa	full board
pianterreno	ground floor
pranzo	lunch
prenotazione	reservation
primo piano	first floor
scale	stairs
spingere	push
tirare	pull
uscita d'emergenza	emergency exit

THINGS YOU'LL HEAR

Mi spiace, siamo al completo
I'm sorry, we're full

Non ci sono più camere singole/doppie
There are no single/double rooms left

Per quante notti?
For how many nights?

Come vuole pagare?
How will you be paying?

Pagamento anticipato, per favore
Please pay in advance

Dovete liberare la stanza entro mezzogiorno
You must vacate the room by midday

CAMPING AND CARAVANNING

Campsites in Italy usually have excellent facilities. Prices differ according to the size of the tent (**casetta** = 'little house', **canadese** = 'two-man tent') and/or the number of people sharing it. You can generally pay for a parking space next to the tent. Moving the car at certain times – mealtimes, for example – is forbidden because it raises dust. If you go out in the evening you will not be allowed to bring your car back inside the site after midnight, but there are often parking facilities just outside.

Most campsites have electric generators. A small daily fee will be added to your bill if you use them. Toilet and washing facilities are generally very good. You may have to pay for a hot shower with coins or tokens that you insert into a machine attached to the shower. If tokens (**gettoni**) are needed, these will be available at the campsite office. Cold showers are free. The campsite office usually acts as a mini-bank as well. You can deposit all your money there and withdraw it on a daily basis. The office will also exchange foreign currency.

USEFUL WORDS AND PHRASES

backpack	lo zaino	*tza-eeno*
bonfire	il falò	*falo*
bucket	il secchio	*sek-yo*
campsite	il campeggio	*kampej-jo*
go camping	andare in campeggio	*andare een kampej-jo*
caravan	la roulotte	*roolot*
caravan site	il campeggio	*kampej-jo*
cooking utensils	gli utensili da cucina	*ootenseelee da koocheena*
drinking water	l'acqua potabile	*akwa pota-beele*
groundsheet	il telone impermeabile	*telone eempair-me abeele*

hitchhike	fare l'autostop	_fare lowto-stop_
rope	la fune, la corda	_foone, korda_
rubbish	l'immondizia	_eem-mondeetzee-a_
saucepans	le pentole	_pentole_
sleeping bag	il sacco a pelo	_sak-ko a pelo_
tent	la tenda	_tenda_
tokens	i gettoni	_jet-tonee_
youth hostel	l'ostello della gioventù	_ostel-lo del-la joventoo_

Can I camp here?
Posso campeggiare qui?
pos-so kampej-jare kwee

Can we park the caravan here?
Possiamo parcheggiare la roulotte qui?
poss-yamo parkej-jare la roolot kwee

Where is the nearest campsite/caravan site?
Qual è il campeggio più vicino?
kwal eh eel kampej-jo p-yoo veecheeno

What is the charge per night?
Quanto si paga per notte?
kwanto see paga pair not-te

I only want to stay for one night
Vorrei fermarmi solo una notte
vor-ray fairmarmee solo oona not-te

How much is it for a week?
Quanto mi viene a costare per una settimana?
kwanto mee v-yene a kostare pair oona set-teemana

We're leaving tomorrow
Partiamo domani
part-yamo domanee

Where is the kitchen?
Dov'è la cucina?
dov<u>e</u>h la kooch<u>ee</u>na

Can I light a fire here?
Posso accendere il fuoco qui?
p<u>o</u>s-so ach<u>e</u>ndaire eel fw<u>o</u>ko kwee

Can I have some tokens for the shower?
Potrei avere alcuni gettoni per la doccia?
p<u>o</u>tray av<u>ai</u>re alk<u>oo</u>nee jet-t<u>o</u>nee pair la d<u>o</u>cha

Where can I get …?
Dove posso trovare …?
d<u>o</u>ve p<u>o</u>s-so trov<u>a</u>re

Is there any drinking water?
C'è acqua potabile?
cheh <u>a</u>kwa pot<u>a</u>-beele

THINGS YOU'LL SEE

acqua potabile	drinking water
a persona	per person
campeggio	campsite
cucina	kitchen
docce	showers
gabinetti	toilets
ostello della gioventù	youth hostel
rimorchio	trailer
roulotte	caravan
tariffa	charge
tenda	tent
vietato accendere fuochi	no campfires
vietato il campeggio	no camping

VILLAS AND APARTMENTS

In Italy you can arrange to rent an apartment through travel agencies or through an estate agent. If you make a reservation, you will be asked to leave a deposit in advance.

When you arrive in the tourist resort where you have reserved the villa or apartment, you will have to sign a contract. Your name, the date of the rental, the address of the apartment, the amount of your deposit etc, will be specified in this contract. You may be asked to pay for certain 'extras' not included in the original price. Gas and electricity are normally included, but cleaning seldom is. It's a good idea to ask about an inventory of goods at the start, rather than be told something is missing just as you are about to leave. Sometimes you will find an inventory in the apartment (in a drawer or cupboard). Usually, you are not required to sign it.

You may be asked for a deposit, in case you break something. Make sure this is specified in the contract you sign. You will get your money back when you leave.

USEFUL WORDS AND PHRASES

bath	la vasca da bagno	v*a*ska da b*a*n-yo
bathroom	il bagno	b*a*n-yo
bedroom	la camera da letto	k*a*maira da l*e*t-to
blocked	intasato	eentaz*a*to
boiler	lo scaldabagno	skaldab*a*n-yo
broken	rotto	r*o*t-to
caretaker	il portinaio	porteen*i*-o
(*female*)	la portinaia	porteen*i*-a
central heating	il riscaldamento centrale	reeskaldam*e*nto chentr*a*le
cleaner	l'uomo delle pulizie	w*o*mo d*e*l-le pooleetz*ee*-e
(*female*)	la donna delle pulizie	d*o*n-na d*e*l-le pooleetz*ee*-e

cooker	il fornello	*fornel-lo*
deposit (*security*)	la cauzione	*kowtz-yone*
(*part payment*)	la caparra	*kapar-ra*
drain	lo scarico	*skareeko*
dustbin	il bidone della spazzatura	*beedone del-la spatzzatoora*
duvet	il piumino	*p-yoomeeno*
electrician	l'elettricista	*elet-treecheesta*
electricity	l'elettricità	*elet-treecheeta*
estate agent	l'agente immobiliare	*ajente eem-mobeelyare*
fridge	il frigorifero	*freegoreefairo*
fusebox	la scatola dei fusibili	*skatola day foozeebeelee*
gas	il gas	*'gas'*
grill	la griglia	*greel-ya*
heater	il termosifone	*tair-mo-see-fone*
iron	il ferro da stiro	*fair-ro da steero*
ironing board	la tavola da stiro	*tavola da steero*
keys	le chiavi	*k-ya-vee*
kitchen	la cucina	*koocheena*
leak (*noun*)	la perdita	*pairdeeta*
(*verb*)	perdere	*pairdaire*
light	la luce	*looche*
living room	il soggiorno	*soj-jorno*
maid	la cameriera	*kamair-yaira*
pillow	il cuscino	*koosheeno*
pillowcase	la federa	*fedaira*
plumber	l'idraulico	*eedrowleeko*
refund	il rimborso	*reemborso*
sheets	le lenzuola	*lentzwola*
shower	la doccia	*docha*
sink	il lavandino	*lavandeeno*
stopcock	il rubinetto d'arresto	*roobeenet-to dar-resto*
swimming pool	la piscina	*peesheena*

tap	il rubinetto	*roobeenet-to*
toilet	il gabinetto	*gabeenet-to*
towel	l'asciugamano	*ashoogamano*
washing machine	la lavatrice	*lavatreeche*
water	l'acqua	*akwa*
water heater	lo scaldabagno	*skalda-ban-yo*

I'd like to rent an apartment/a villa for … days
Vorrei affittare un appartamento/una villa per … giorni
vor-ray af-feet-tare oon ap-partamento/oona veel-la pair … jornee

Do I have to pay a deposit?
Devo versare una cauzione?
devo vairsare oona kowtz-yone

Does the price include gas and electricity?
Il gas e l'elettricità sono inclusi nel prezzo?
eel 'gas' ay lelet-treecheeta sono eenkloozee nel pretzo

Where is this item?
Dove si trova questo oggetto?
dove see trova kwesto oj-jet-to

Please take it off the inventory
Lo tolga dall'inventario, per favore
lo tolga dal-leenventar-yo pair favore

We've broken this
Abbiamo rotto questo
abb-yamo rot-to kwesto

This was broken when we arrived
Era già rotto quando siamo arrivati
era ja rot-to kwando s-yamo ar-reevatee

This was missing when we arrived
Non c'era quando siamo arrivati
non chera kwando s-yamo ar-reevatee

Can I have my deposit back?
Potrei riavere la cauzione?
potray ree-avaire la kowtz-yone

Can we have an extra bed?
Potremmo avere un letto in più?
potrem-mo avaire oon let-to een p-yoo

Can we have more crockery/cutlery?
Potremmo avere ancora un po' di stoviglie/posate?
potrem-mo avaire ankora oon po dee stoveel-ye/pozate

When does the maid come?
Quando viene la cameriera?
kwando v-yene la kamair-yaira

Where can I buy/find …?
Dove posso comprare/trovare …?
dove pos-so komprare/trovare

How does the water heater work?
Come funziona lo scaldabagno?
kome foontz-yona lo skalda-ban-yo

Do you do ironing/baby-sitting?
Sa stirare/badare ai bambini?
sa steerare/badare i bambeenee

Do you prepare lunch/dinner?
È in grado di preparare il pranzo/la cena?
eh een grado dee preparare eel prantzo/la chena

Do we have to pay extra or is it included?
Dobbiamo pagarlo a parte o è incluso nel prezzo?
dobb-yamo pagarlo a parte o eh eenkloozo nel pret-zo

The shower doesn't work
La doccia non funziona
la docha non foontz-yona

The sink is blocked
Il lavandino è intasato
eel lavandeeno eh eentazato

The sink/toilet is leaking
Il lavandino/gabinetto perde
eel lavandeeno/gabeenet-to pairde

There's a burst pipe
Si è rotto un tubo
see eh rot-to oon toobo

The rubbish has not been collected for a week
Non portano via la spazzatura da una settimana
non portano vee-a la spatz-zatoora da oona set-teemana

There's no electricity/gas/water
Non c'è elettricità/gas/acqua
non cheh elet-treecheeta/'gas'/akwa

Can you mend it today?
Può ripararlo oggi?
pwo reepararlo oj-jee

Send your bill to …
Mandi il conto a …
mandee eel konto a

I'm staying at …
Sto a …
sto a

Thank you for everything!
Grazie di tutto!
gratzee-e dee toot-to

See you again next year!
Al prossimo anno!
al pros-seemo an-no

DRIVING

In Italy you drive on the right and overtake on the left. On dual carriageways you may stay in the left-hand lane if heavy traffic has taken over the right-hand lane. Normally, you may move from the right- to the left-hand lane only for turning or overtaking. On three-lane roads with traffic flowing in both directions, the central lane is for overtaking only.

At junctions where there are no road signs or traffic lights, you must give way to traffic coming from the right, except in the case of a service station exit, a private road, or a track entering the main road. Usually, a diamond-shaped yellow sign tells you that you have the right of way. The end of this right of way is indicated by a similar sign with a bar through it. An upside-down red triangle or a 'STOP' sign means that you must give way to all vehicles coming from both the right and the left.

In built-up areas the speed limit is 50 km/h (31 mph). On open roads (if not otherwise indicated) it is 90 km/h (56 mph), and on motorways it is 130 km/h (81 mph).

If you break down and are forced to stop in the middle of the road, you must place a red triangle 50 metres (about 160 feet) behind your vehicle to warn other drivers. All drivers must carry this triangle, which can be rented from the offices of the **ACI (Automobile Club Italiano)** when you enter Italy and then returned when you leave the country.

There are emergency telephones on most highways. If you break down on the **Autostrada del Sole** (Milan–Rome) or on other motorways, there are emergency telephones on the right side of the road at intervals of 1 or 2 km. Generally, it is illegal to walk along the motorway or hitchhike but, if the breakdown occurs between two telephones, you are allowed to walk to the next emergency phone. (Also see Emergencies, page 107.)

Most towns have shopping centres and, if you park where you are not supposed to, your car will be towed away. You should park either in a free parking area or in a paying car park or garage. Charges are displayed on a sign in the car park.

You'll be given a parking ticket when you arrive or, if there is a car park attendant, he or she will place a ticket on your windscreen and you pay on departure.

SOME COMMON ROAD SIGNS

accendere i fari	headlights on
attenzione	watch out, caution
autostrada	motorway (with toll)
banchina non transitabile	soft verge
caduta massi	falling rocks
centro	town centre
code	traffic ahead
controllo automatico della velocità	automatic speed monitor
cunetta o dosso	ditch
deviazione	diversion
disporsi su due file	two-lane traffic
divieto di accesso	no entry
divieto di fermata	no stopping
divieto di transito	no thoroughfare
dogana	customs
escluso residenti	residents only
fine del tratto autostradale	end of motorway
ghiaccio	ice
incrocio	junction
incrocio pericoloso	dangerous junction/ crossroads
informazioni turistiche	tourist information
lavori in corso	roadworks
nebbia	fog
non oltrepassare	no trespassing
pagare qui	pay here
parcheggio a giorni alterni	parking on alternate days
parcheggio a pagamento	paying car park

→

parcheggio custodito	car park with attendant
parcheggio incustodito	unattended car park
pedaggio	toll
pedoni	pedestrians
pericolo	danger
pista ciclabile	bicycle trail
rallentare	reduce speed
scuola	school
senso unico	one way
sosta vietata	no parking
sottopassaggio	subway
strada a fondo cieco	dead end
strada camionabile	route for heavy vehicles
strada ghiacciata	ice on road
strada statale	main road
strada sdrucciolevole	slippery road
strada secondaria	secondary road
strada statale	main road
uscita camion	works exit
veicoli lenti	slow lane
zona a traffico limitato	restricted traffic area
zona pedonale	shopping centre

USEFUL WORDS AND PHRASES

automatic	con il cambio automatico	*kon eel kam-bee-o owtomateeko*
bonnet	il cofano	*kofano*
boot	il portabagagli	*portabagal-yee*
brake	il freno	*freno*
breakdown	il guasto	*gwasto*
car	l'automobile, la macchina	*owtomobeele, mak-keena*
car ferry	il traghetto	*traget-to*
car park	il parcheggio	*parkej-jo*
clutch	la frizione	*freetz-yone*

crossroads	l'incrocio	*eenkrocho*
drive	guidare	*gweedare*
engine	il motore	*motore*
exhaust	lo scappamento	*skap-pamento*
fanbelt	la cinghia della ventola	*cheeng-ya del-la ventola*
garage *(for repairs)*	l'autorimessa	*owtoreemes-sa*
gear	il cambio, la marcia	*kam-bee-o, marcha*
gears	le marce	*marche*
headlights	i fari	*faree*
indicator	la freccia	*frech-cha*
junction	l'incrocio	*eenkrocho*
(motorway entry)	raccordo di entrata	*rak-kordo dee entrata*
(motorway exit)	raccordo di uscita	*rak-kordo dee oosheeta*
licence	la patente	*patente*
lorry	il camion, l'autocarro	*kam-yon, owtokar-ro*
manual	con il cambio manuale	*kon eel kam-bee-o manwale*
mirror	lo specchietto	*spekk-yet-to*
motorcycle	la motocicletta	*motocheeklet-ta*
motorway	l'autostrada	*owtostrada*
number plate	la targa	*targa*
petrol	la benzina	*bendzeena*
petrol station	la stazione di servizio	*statz-yone dee sairveetz-yo*
rear lights	i fari posteriori	*faree postair-yoree*
ring road	raccordo anulare	*rak-kordo anoolare*
road	la strada	*strada*
spare parts	i pezzi di ricambio	*petzee dee reekam-bee-o*
spark plug	la candela	*kandela*
speed	la velocità	*velocheeta*

speed limit	il limite di velocità	_leemeete dee velocheeta_
speedometer	il tachimetro	_takeemetro_
steering wheel	il volante	_volante_
traffic lights	il semaforo	_semaforo_
trailer	il rimorchio, la roulotte	_reemork-yo, roolot_
transmission	la scatola del cambio	_skatola dek kam-bee-o_
tyre	la gomma	_gom-ma_
van	il furgone	_foorgone_
warning sign	il triangolo	_tree-angolo_
wheel	la ruota	_rwota_
windscreen	il parabrezza	_parabretza_
windscreen wiper	il tergicristallo	_tairjee-kreestal-lo_

Could you check the oil/water level, please?
Potrebbe controllare il livello dell'olio/dell'acqua, per favore?
potreb-be kontrol-lare eel leevel-lo del ol-yo/del akwa pair favore

Fill it up, please!
Faccia il pieno, per favore
facha eel p-yeno pair favore

I'd like 35 litres of 4-star petrol, please
Mi dia trentacinque litri di super, per favore
mee dee-a trentacheenkwe leetree dee soopair pair favore

Do you do repairs?
Effettua riparazioni?
ef-fet-too-a reeparatz-yonee

Can you repair the clutch?
Può ripararmi la frizione?
pwo reepararmee la freetz-yone

There is something wrong with the engine
C'è qualcosa che non va nel motore
cheh kwalkoza ke non va nel motore

The engine is overheating
Il motore si surriscalda
eel motore see soor-reeskalda

I need a new tyre
Ho bisogno di una gomma nuova
o beezon-yo dee oona gom-ma nwova

Can you replace this?
Può sostituirlo?
pwo sosteetoo-eerlo

The indicator is not working
La freccia non funziona
la frech-cha non foontz-yona

How long will it take?
Quanto tempo ci vorrà?
kwanto tempo chee vor-ra

Where can I park?
Dove posso parcheggiare?
dove pos-so parkej-jare

I'd like to hire a car
Vorrei noleggiare una macchina
vor-ray nolej-jare oona mak-keena

I'd like an automatic/a manual
Vorrei una macchina con il cambio automatico/manuale
vor-ray oona mak-keena kon eel kam-bee-o owtomateeko/manwale

How much is it for one day?
Quanto costa per un giorno?
kwanto kosta pair oon jorno

Is there a mileage charge?
C'è un supplemento per il chilometraggio?
cheh oon soop-plemento pair eel keelometraj-jo

When do I have to return it?
Quando devo riportarla?
kwando devo reeportarla

Where is the nearest petrol station?
Dov'è la stazione di servizio più vicina?
doveh la statz-yone dee sairveetz-yo p-yoo veecheena

How do I get to …?
Può dirmi come andare a …?
pwo deermee kome andare a

Is this the road to …?
È questa la strada per …?
eh kwesta la strada pair

Which is the quickest way to …?
Qual è la strada più breve per …?
kwal eh la strada p-yoo breve pair

THINGS YOU'LL SEE

acqua	water
area di servizio	service area
aspirapolvere	vacuum cleaner
autolavaggio	car wash
autorimessa	garage (for repairs)
benzina	petrol
benzina senza piombo	unleaded petrol
benzina super	4-star petrol
casello autostradale	motorway toll booth
cera per auto	car wax
code	traffic queue
deviazione	diversion
gasolio	diesel oil
gommista	tyre repairs
guidare a passo d'uomo	drive at walking speed

→

liquido tergicristallo	windscreen washer liquid
olio	oil
raccordo autostradale	motorway junction
spegnere il motore	turn off engine
spingere	push
stazione di servizio	service station
tirare	pull
uscita	exit
vietato fumare	no smoking

THINGS YOU'LL HEAR

Vuole una macchina con il cambio automatico o manuale?
Would you like an automatic or a manual?

Esibisca la patente, per favore
May I see your licence, please?

Mi fa vedere il passaporto, per favore?
May I see your passport, please?

DIRECTIONS YOU MAY BE GIVEN

a destra	right
a sinistra	left
dritto	straight on
giri a destra	turn right
giri a sinistra	turn left
il primo/la prima a destra	first on the right
il secondo/la seconda a sinistra	second on the left
vada oltre ...	go past the ...

TRAVELLING AROUND

Rail Travel

Rail travel is so inexpensive in Italy that it is very widely used. During the holiday season, travelling by train can be difficult, so, wherever possible, you should reserve your seat well in advance. Children under four years of age not occupying a seat travel free, and there is a half-price fare for children between four and twelve years old. Considerable reductions are available for families and individuals on short-term season tickets. Sleeping cars are available on most domestic long-distance night services, and most long-distance trains have restaurant cars. On shorter journeys there will be a trolley from which you can buy sandwiches and soft drinks. In main stations, platform vendors pass by the train windows.

Trains on Italian State Railways (**Ferrovie dello Stato** or **FS**) are classified as follows:

EC (**Eurocity**): very fast international train, with first and second class compartments. A supplement must be paid in advance, but there is no charge for booking a seat in advance.
IC (**Intercity**): very fast national train. Most **IC**s have first and second classes, but there are still a few with first class only. It's best to check this before departure. A supplement must be paid in advance, but reserving a seat is free.
Espresso: long-distance fast train. No supplement required.
Diretto: long-distance train stopping at main stations.
Regionale: small local train stopping at nearly every station.

You should find out in advance whether you will be taking an **IC** or **EC** train and ask to pay the supplement when you buy your ticket. If you have a return ticket, you should validate it by stamping the date on both the outward bound and return parts on the day you travel. In most stations, there are ticket-stamping machines but, in small stations, you should go to the ticket office.

Long-Distance Bus Travel

People do travel long distances by bus in Italy but trains are not expensive and are quicker. Local buses for small towns and places of interest are generally inexpensive and run frequently. The long-distance buses often have a system similar to that of local buses: when you enter, you stamp your ticket in the ticket-stamping machine.

Local Public Transport

In large cities there are several types of public transport: bus, trolley bus (**filobus**), tram and underground (**Metropolitana**). In some cities there is an integrated public transport system, which means that the same tickets can be used on all types of transport. Tickets are inexpensive and operate on a flat-fare basis. In most cities, they are valid for 60 to 75 minutes, but in some they are only valid for a one-way trip. Tickets can be bought in the underground, at any newspaper kiosk, **tabaccaio**, or ordinary bar with a '**vendita biglietti**' sign in the window.

 When you enter a bus, **filobus** etc, you must insert your ticket into a machine that stamps the time on it. The only restriction is that you cannot re-enter the **Metropolitana** with the same ticket, even if you have not yet used up your 75 minutes. There are inspectors who make random checks and, if you are travelling without a valid ticket, you can expect an on-the-spot fine of about 25 euros. In most places public transport is quick and efficient. Smoking is forbidden on all local public transport.

Taxi and Boat

It is advisable not to travel in a taxi that does not have the 'taxi' sign on top. Taxis without this sign are private taxis and may charge astronomical prices. The marked taxis are reliable and efficient, but they do have a high minimum charge. There is also an extra charge for each item of luggage and for rides at night.

In Venice (where, of course, there are no buses etc) you travel by **vaporetto**, a small passenger boat. You must buy your ticket in advance from the kiosk at **vaporetti** stops. There is a flat fare for all destinations. However, there are special offers such as 24-hour tickets with which you can travel on any number of boats for any distance, starting from the time when you stamp your ticket at the boat stop (not from when you buy it).

USEFUL WORDS AND PHRASES

adult	l'adulto	_adoolto_
airport	l'aeroporto	_a-airoporto_
airport bus	l'autobus per l'aeroporto	_owtoboos pair la-airoporto_
aisle seat	il posto vicino al corridoio	_posto veecheeno al kor-reedo-yo_
baggage claim	il ritiro bagagli	_reeteero bagal-yee_
berth _(on a boat)_	la cuccetta	_kooch-chet-ta_
boarding pass	la carta d'imbarco	_karta deembarko_
boat	la barca,	_barka,_
	il battello	_bat-telo_
booking office	la biglietteria	_beel-yet-teree-a_
buffet	il buffet	_boofe_
bus	l'autobus	_owtoboos_
(coach)	la corriera	_kor-ree-aira_
bus station	la stazione degli autobus	_statz-yone del-yee owtoboos_
bus stop	la fermata dell'autobus	_fermata del lowtoboos_
carry-on luggage	il bagaglio a mano	_bagal-yo a mano_
check-in desk	l'accettazione (bagagli)	_achet-tatz-yone bagal-yee_
child	il bambino	_bambeeno_
(female)	la bambina	_bambeena_
compartment	lo scompartimento	_skomparteemento_
connection	la coincidenza	_ko-eencheedentza_

cruise	la crociera	*krochaira*
customs	la dogana	*dogana*
departure lounge	la sala d'attesa	*sala dat-teza*
domestic	nazionale	*natz-yonale*
emergency exit	l'uscita di sicurezza	*oosheeta dee seekooretza*
entrance	l'entrata	*entrata*
exit	l'uscita	*oosheeta*
fare	la tariffa	*tareef-fa*
ferry	il traghetto	*trag-et-to*
first class	la prima classe	*preema klas-se*
flight	il volo	*volo*
flight number	il numero del volo	*noomairo del volo*
gate	l'uscita	*oosheeta*
international	internazionale	*eentairnatz-yonale*
lost property office	l'ufficio oggetti smarriti	*oof-feecho ojet-tee zmar-reetee*
luggage trolley	il carrello	*kar-rel-lo*
luggage room	il deposito bagagli	*depozeeto bagal-yee*
network map	la piantina dei trasporti pubblici	*p-yanteena day tras-portee poob-bleechee*
nonsmoking	non fumatori	*non foomatoree*
number 5 bus	l'autobus numero cinque	*owtoboos noomero cheenkwe*
passport	il passaporto	*pas-saporto*
platform	il binario	*beenaree-o*
railway	la ferrovia	*fer-rovee-a*
reserved seat	il posto riservato	*posto ree-sairvato*
restaurant car	il vagone ristorante	*vagone reestorante*
return ticket	il biglietto di andata e ritorno	*beel-yet-to dee andata ay reetorno*
seat	il posto	*posto*
second class	la seconda classe	*sekonda klas-se*
single ticket	il biglietto di sola andata	*beel-yet-to dee sola andata*

sleeping car	il vagone letto	*vagone let-to*
smoking	fumatori	*foomatoree*
station	la stazione	*statz-yone*
subway	il sottopassaggio	*sot-topas-saj-jo*
taxi	il taxi	*'taxi'*
terminal	il capolinea	*kapoleene-a*
ticket	il biglietto	*beel-yet-to*
timetable	l'orario	*orar-yo*
train	il treno	*treno*
tram	il tram	*'tram'*
trolley bus	il filobus	*feeloboos*
underground	la metropolitana	*metro-poleetana*
waiting room	la sala d'attesa	*sala dat-teza*
window seat	il posto vicino al	*posto veecheeno al*
	finestrino	*feenestreeno*

AIR TRAVEL

I'd like a non-smoking seat, please
Vorrei un posto per non fumatori, per favore
vor-ray oon posto pair non foomatoree pair favore

I'd like a window seat, please
Vorrei un posto vicino al finestrino
vor-ray oon posto veecheeno al feenestreeno

How long will the flight be delayed?
Con quanto ritardo partirà il volo?
kon kwanto reetardo parteera eel volo

Which gate for the flight to …?
Qual è l'uscita del volo per …?
kwal eh loosheeta del volo pair

TRAIN AND BUS TRAVEL

When does the train/bus for Florence leave?
A che ora parte il treno/l'autobus per Firenze?
a ke ora parte eel treno/lowtoboos pair feerentze

When does the train/bus from Rome arrive?
A che ora arriva il treno/l'autobus da Roma?
a ke ora ar-reeva eel treno/lowtoboos da roma

When is the next train/bus to Venice?
A che ora c'è il prossimo treno/autobus per Venezia?
a ke ora cheh eel pros-seemo treno/owtoboos pair venetzee-a

When is the first/last train/bus to Turin?
A che ora c'è il primo/l'ultimo treno/autobus per Torino?
a ke ora cheh eel preemo/loolteemo treno/owtoboos pair toreeno

What is the fare to Naples?
Quanto costa il biglietto per Napoli?
kwanto kosta eel beel-yet-to pair napolee

Do I have to change?
Devo cambiare?
devo kamb-yare

Does the train/bus stop at Padua?
Il treno/l'autobus ferma a Padova?
eel treno/lowtoboos fairma a padova

How long does it take to get to Trieste?
Quanto tempo ci mette per arrivare a Trieste?
kwanto tempo chee met-te pair ar-ree-varai a tree-este

Where can I buy a ticket?
Dove posso comprare il biglietto?
dove pos-so komprare eel beel-yet-to

Could you help me get a ticket?
Potrebbe aiutarmi a comprare il biglietto?
potreb-be i-ootarmee a comp-rarai eel beel-yet-to

A single/return ticket to Bologna, please
Un biglietto di sola andata/di andata e ritorno per Bologna,
   per favore
*oon beel-yet-to dee sola andata/dee andata ay reetorno pair
   bolon-ya pair favore*

Do I have to pay a supplement?
Devo pagare un supplemento?
devo pagare oon soop-plemento

I'd like to reserve a seat
Vorrei prenotare un posto a sedere
vor-ray prenotare oon posto a sedere

Is this the right train/bus for Genoa?
È questo il treno/l'autobus per Genova?
eh kwesto eel treno/lowtoboos pair jenova

Is this the right platform for the Palermo train?
È questo il binario del treno per Palermo?
eh kwesto eel beenaree-o del treno pair palairmo

Which platform for the Perugia train?
Da che binario parte il treno per Perugia?
da ke beenaree-o parte eel treno pair perooja

Is the train/bus late?
Il treno/l'autobus è in ritardo?
eel treno/lowtoboos eh een reetardo

Could you help me with my luggage, please?
Potrebbe darmi una mano con i bagagli, per favore?
potreb-be darmee oona mano kon ee bagal-yee pair favore

Is this a non-smoking compartment?
È uno scompartimento non fumatori?
eh oono skomparteemento non foomatoree

Is this seat free?
È libero questo posto?
eh leebairo kwesto posto

This seat is taken
Questo posto è occupato
kwesto posto eh ok-koopato

I have reserved this seat
Questo posto è riservato
kwesto posto eh ree-sairvato

May I open/close the window?
Posso aprire/chiudere il finestrino?
pos-so apreere/k-yoodaire eel feenestreeno

When do we arrive in Bari?
A che ora arriviamo a Bari?
a ke ora arreev-yamo a baree

What station is this?
Che stazione è questa?
ke statz-yone eh kwesta

Do we stop at Pisa?
Ci fermiamo a Pisa?
chee fairmee-amo a peeza

Is there a restaurant car on this train?
C'è un vagone ristorante su questo treno?
cheh oon vagone reestorante soo kwesto treno

LOCAL PUBLIC TRANSPORT

Where is the nearest underground station?
Qual è la stazione della metropolitana più vicina?
kwal eh la statz-yone del-la metro-poleetana p-yoo veecheena

Where is the bus station?
Dov'è la stazione degli autobus/delle corriere?
doveh la statz-yone del-yee owtoboos/delle cor-riere

Which buses go to Mantua?
Quale autobus va a Mantova?
kwale owtoboos va a mantova

How often do the buses to San Gimignano run?
Ogni quanto passa l'autobus per San Gimignano?
on-yee kwanto pas-sa lowtoboos pair san jeemeen-yano

Will you let me know when we're there?
Mi potrebbe avvertire quando arriviamo là?
mee potreb-be av-verteere kwando ar-reev-yamo la

Do I have to get off yet?
Devo scendere qui?
devo shendaire kwee

How do you get to Asti?
Come posso andare ad Asti?
kome pos-so andare ad astee

I want to go to Udine
Voglio andare a Udine
vol-yo andare a oodeene

Do you go near Enna?
Passa vicino ad Enna?
pas-sa veecheeno ad en-na

TAXI AND BOAT

To the airport, please
All'aeroporto, per favore
alla-airoporto pair favore

How much will it cost?
Quanto mi verrà a costare?
kwanto mee vair-ra a kostare

Please stop here
Si fermi qui, per favore
see fairmee kwee pair favore

Could you wait here for me and take me back?
Può aspettarmi qui per riportarmi indietro?
pwo aspet-tarmee kwee pair reeportarmee eend-yetro

Where can I get the boat to Sirmione?
Dove posso prendere il battello per Sirmione?
dove pos-so prendaire eel bat-tello pair seerm-yone

THINGS YOU'LL SEE

abbonamento mensile	monthly ticket
abbonamento settimanale	weekly ticket
ai binari/treni	to the platforms/trains
arrivi	arrivals
bambini	children
biglietto	ticket
biglietto d'accesso ai treni	platform ticket
biglietto giornaliero	day ticket
biglietto valido per più corse	multi-journey ticket
cambiare	to change (transportation)
cambio	exchange office
capolinea	terminal
carrozza	carriage, car
controllo bagagli	luggage control
controllo biglietti	ticket inspection
controllo passaporti	passport control
cuccetta	sleeping car
deposito bagagli	left luggage
diretto	long-distance train
discesa	exit
distributore automatico di biglietti	ticket machine
entrata	entrance/entry
è pericoloso sporgersi	it is dangerous to lean out
espresso	long-distance fast train

→

fermata	stop
Ferrovie dello Stato/FS	State Railway
fumatori	smoking
giro in barca	boat trip
informazioni	information
la domenica	Sundays
la domenica e i giorni festivi	Sundays and holidays
libero	free
macchina obliteratrice	ticket-stamping machine
nazionale	domestic
non ferma a …	does not stop at …
non fumatori	non-smoking
non parlare al conducente	do not speak to the driver
occupato	occupied, reserved
oggetti smarriti	lost property
ogni abuso sarà punito con …	penalty for misuse …
ora locale	local time
orario	timetable
orario di volo	flight time
partenze	departures
passeggeri	passengers
percorso	route
porto	harbour, port
posti in piedi	standing room
posto (a sedere)	seat
posto prenotato	reserved seat
rapido	fast train
riservato ai non fumatori	non-smokers only
ritardo	delay
ritiro bagagli	baggage claim
sala d'attesa	waiting room
(segnale d')allarme	emergency alarm
solo il sabato/la domenica	Saturdays/Sundays only
spuntini, panini	snacks, sandwiches
supplemento rapido	supplement for fast train
tesserino	travel card

→

tragitto breve	short journey
uscita	exit
uscita di sicurezza	emergency exit
vagone	carriage, car
vagone letto	sleeping car
vagone ristorante	restaurant car
viaggio	trip
vietato fumare	no smoking
vietato l'ingresso	no entry
vietato sporgersi	do not lean out
volo	flight
volo di linea	scheduled flight

Things You'll Hear

Ha bagagli?
Do you have any luggage?

Fumatori o non fumatori?
Smoking or non-smoking?

Posto vicino al corridoio o vicino al finestrino?
Window seat or aisle seat?

Posso vedere il vostro passaporto/biglietto, per favore?
Can I see your passport/ticket, please?

I passeggeri in partenza per Roma sono pregati di recarsi all'imbarco
Passengers for Rome are requested to board

Recarsi all'uscita quattro, per favore
Please proceed to gate number four

Biglietti, prego
Tickets, please

Il prossimo treno parte alle diciotto
The next train leaves at 18.00

Deve cambiare a Firenze
Change at Florence

Deve pagare un supplemento
You must pay a supplement

Non ci sono più posti per Catania
There are no more seats available for Catania

Il treno intercity numero 687 per Roma è in partenza dal binario tre
Intercity train number 687 for Rome is leaving from
  platform three

Il treno regionale numero 89 da Bologna è in arrivo al binario due
Local train number 89 from Bologna is approaching
  platform two

Il treno espresso numero 435 da Venezia viaggia con trenta minuti di ritardo
Express train number 435 from Venice is running thirty
  minutes late

Apra la valigia, per favore
Open your suitcase, please

EATING OUT

There are various types of places in which to eat in Italy. For
snacks, the most common is the bar. These are open all day
from early morning until about 10 pm. They are all licensed to
sell alcohol and usually offer a variety of sandwiches, rolls,
cakes, and hot and cold drinks. In most bars you are required
to first go to the cashier, place your order, pay and get a receipt
(**scontrino**). Then hand the receipt to the bartender and repeat
your order. You will notice that most Italians stand up in bars
– sitting down costs extra. The sign **tavola calda** means that
hot dishes are also served.

For full meals there are **osteria**, **pizzeria**, **trattoria**, **taverna**
and **ristorante**. Wherever possible, it's a good idea to choose
the **menu turistico** (tourist menu) or the **menu fisso** (set
menu). Although the variety is more restricted, the food is of
the same standard and you get a good deal more for your
money, without having to face any service charge shocks at the
end of the meal. Always ask for the local culinary specialities
and local wine. These are generally excellent, and wine is less
expensive and of superior quality in its place of origin.

In Italy, you can order the following types of coffee: **espresso**
(small, strong, black coffee), **caffè macchiato** (espresso with a
dash of milk), **cappuccino** (frothy, milky coffee sprinkled with
cocoa), **caffelatte** (coffee with milk). These are the most common,
but there is also **caffè corretto** (espresso with a liqueur), **caffè
decaffeinato** (decaffeinated coffee), **caffè lungo** (weak espresso)
and **caffè ristretto** (strong espresso). Remember that if you ask
for '**Un caffè, per favore**', you will be served an **espresso**.

USEFUL WORDS AND PHRASES

beer	la birra	_beer_-ra
bill	il conto	_konto_
bottle	la bottiglia	bot-_teel_-ya
bread	il pane	_pane_

butter	il burro	*boor-ro*
café	il bar	*bar*
cake	la torta	*torta*
carafe	la caraffa	*karaf-fa*
child's portion	una porzione per bambini	*portz-yone pair bambeenee*
coffee	il caffè	*kaf-feh*
cup	la tazza	*tatza*
dessert	il dessert	*desser*
fork	la forchetta	*forket-ta*
glass	il bicchiere	*beek-yaire*
half litre	da mezzo litro	*da metzo leetro*
knife	il coltello	*koltel-lo*
litre	un litro	*leetro*
main course	il piatto principale	*p-yat-to preencheepale*
menu	il menù	*menoo*
milk	il latte	*lat-te*
napkin	il tovagliolo	*toval-yolo*
pepper	il pepe	*pepey*
plate	il piatto	*p-yat-to*
receipt (*in bars*)	lo scontrino	*skontreeno*
(*in restaurants*)	la ricevuta	*reechevoota*
restaurant	il ristorante	*reestorante*
salt	il sale	*sale*
sandwich	il panino	*paneeno*
snack	lo spuntino	*spoonteeno*
soup	la minestra	*meenestra*
spoon	il cucchiaio	*kook-ya-yo*
starter	l'antipasto	*anteepasto*
sugar	lo zucchero	*dzookairo*
table	il tavolo	*tavolo*
tea	il tè	*teh*
teaspoon	il cucchiaino	*kook-ya-eeno*
tip	la mancia	*mancha*
waiter	il cameriere	*kamair-yaire*
waitress	la cameriera	*kamair-yaira*

water	l'acqua	*akwa*
wine	il vino	*veeno*
wine list	la lista dei vini	*leesta day veenee*

A table for one/two/three, please
Un tavolo per una persona/per due/per tre, per favore
oon tavolo pair oona pairsona/pair doo-e/pair tray pair favore

Is there a highchair?
Si può avere un seggiolone?
see pwo avaire oon seg-gee-olone

Can I see the menu/wine list?
Potrei vedere il menu/la lista dei vini?
potray vedaire eel menoo/la leesta day veenee

What would you recommend?
Cosa ci consiglia?
koza chee konseel-ya

I'd like …
Vorrei …
vor-ray

Just an espresso/cappuccino/coffee with milk, please
Solo un caffè/un cappuccino/un caffelatte, per favore
solo oon kaf-feh/oon kap-poocheeno/oon kaf-felat-te pair favore

I only want a snack
Vorrei solo uno spuntino
vor-ray solo oono spoonteeno

Is there a set menu?
C'è un menù fisso?
cheh oon menoo fees-so

Can we try a local speciality/wine?
Potremmo assaggiare una specialità/un vino locale?
potrem-mo as-saj-jare oona spech-yaleeta/oon veeno lokale

A litre of house red, please
Un litro di vino rosso della casa, per favore
oon leetro dee veeno ros-so del-la kaza pair favore

I'm vegetarian
Sono vegetariano
sono vejetar-yano

Do you have any vegetarian dishes?
Avete piatti vegetariani?
avete p-yat-tee vejetar-yanee

Do you have a vegetarian menu?
Avete un menu vegetariano?
avete oon menoo vejetar-yano

Is this suitable for vegetarians?
Questo è adatto per i vegetariani?
kwesto eh adat-to pair ee vejetar-yanee

I'm allergic to nuts/shellfish
Sono allergico/a alle noci/ai frutti di mare
sono al-lairjeeko/a al-lai nochee/aee froot-tee dee marai

Could we have some water?
Potremmo avere un po' d'acqua?
potrem-mo avaire oon po dakwa

Is there a children's menu?
C'è un menù per bambini?
cheh oon menoo pair bambeenee

Do you do children's portions?
Fate porzioni per bambini?
fatai porzeeonee pair bambeenee

Can you warm this bottle/baby food for me?
Mi può riscaldare il biberon/il pasto del bambino?
mee pwo reeskaldarai eel bee-bairon/eel pazto del bambeeno

Waiter/waitress!
Cameriere/cameriera!
kamair-y<u>ai</u>re/kamair-y<u>ai</u>ra

We didn't order this!
Non lo abbiamo ordinato!
non lo abb-y<u>a</u>mo ordeen<u>a</u>to

You've forgotten to bring my dessert
Ha dimenticato di portarmi il dessert
a deementeek<u>a</u>to dee port<u>a</u>rmee eel dess<u>e</u>r

May we have some more ...?
Potremmo avere ancora un po' di ...?
potr<u>e</u>m-mo av<u>ai</u>re ank<u>o</u>ra oon po dee

Can I have another knife/spoon?
Potrei avere un altro coltello/cucchiaio?
potr<u>ay</u> av<u>ai</u>re oon <u>a</u>ltro kolt<u>e</u>l-lo/kook-y<u>a</u>-yo

Can we have the bill, please?
Può portarci il conto, per favore?
pwo port<u>a</u>rchee eel k<u>o</u>nto pair fav<u>o</u>re

Could I have a receipt, please?
Potrei avere la ricevuta/lo scontrino, per favore?
potr<u>ay</u> av<u>ai</u>re la reechev<u>oo</u>ta/lo skontr<u>ee</u>no pair fav<u>o</u>re

---

> ## THINGS YOU'LL HEAR
>
> **Buon appetito!**
> Enjoy your meal!
>
> **Cosa vuole da bere?**
> What would you like to drink?
>
> **Avete mangiato bene?**
> Did you enjoy your meal?

MENU GUIDE

abbacchio alla romana	Roman-style spring lamb
acciughe sott'olio	anchovies in oil
aceto	vinegar
acqua	water
acqua minerale gassata	sparkling mineral water
acqua minerale non gassata	still mineral water
acqua naturale	still mineral water, tap water
affettato misto	variety of cold, sliced meats such as salami, cooked ham etc
affogato al caffè	ice cream with hot espresso poured over it
aglio	garlic
agnello	lamb
agnello al forno	roast lamb
albicocche	apricots
ananas	pineapple
anatra	duck
anatra all'arancia	duck in orange sauce
anguilla in umido	stewed eel
anguria	watermelon
antipasti	starters
antipasti misti	variety of starters
aperitivo	aperitif
aragosta	lobster
arancia	orange
aranciata	orangeade
aringa	herring
arista di maiale al forno	roast chine of pork
arrosto di tacchino	roast turkey
arrosto di vitello	roast veal
asparagi	asparagus
avocado all'agro	avocado pears with oil and lemon or vinegar
baccalà	dried cod
baccalà alla vicentina	Vicentine-style dried cod
bagnacauda	vegetables (usually raw) in an oil, garlic, and anchovy sauce
barbaresco	dry, red wine from the Piedmont region

barbera	dry, red wine from Piedmont
bardolino	dry red wine from area around Verona
barolo	dark, dry red wine from Piedmont
basilico	basil
bavarese	ice-cream cake with cream
bel paese	soft, high-fat white cheese
besciamella	white sauce
bignè	cream puff
birra	beer
birra chiara	light beer, lager
birra grande	large beer (approx 1 pint)
birra piccola	small beer (approx ½ pint)
birra scura	dark beer
bistecca (di manzo)	steak
bistecca ai ferri	grilled steak
bollito misto con verdure	assorted boiled meats with vegetables
braciola di maiale	pork steak
branzino al forno	baked sea bass
brasato	braised beef with herbs
bresaola	dried, salted beef sliced thinly, and eaten cold with oil and lemon
brioche	type of croissant
brodo	clear broth
brodo di pollo	chicken broth
brodo vegetale	clear vegetable broth
budino	pudding
burro	butter
burro di acciughe	anchovy butter
caciotta	tender, white, medium-fat cheese from Central Italy
caffè	coffee
caffè corretto	espresso with a dash of liqueur
caffè lungo	weak espresso
caffè macchiato	espresso with a dash of milk
caffè ristretto	strong espresso
caffelatte	half coffee, half hot milk
calamari in umido	stewed squid
calamaro	squid
calzone	folded pizza with tomato and mozzarella or ricotta inside

camomilla	camomile tea
cannella	cinnamon
cannelloni al forno	rolls of egg pasta stuffed with meat and baked in the oven
cappelle di funghi porcini alla griglia	grilled boletus mushroom caps
cappuccino	espresso coffee with foaming milk and a sprinkling of cocoa powder
capretto al forno	roast kid
carciofi	artichokes
carciofini sott'olio	baby artichokes in oil
carne	meat
carote	carrots
carpaccio	finely-sliced beef fillets with oil, lemon and grated parmesan
carré di maiale al forno	roast pork loin
cassata siciliana	Sicilian ice-cream cake with glacé fruit, chocolate and ricotta
castagne	chestnuts
cavoletti di Bruxelles	Brussels sprouts
cavolfiore	cauliflower
cavolo	cabbage
cefalo	mullet
cernia	grouper (fish)
charlotte	ice-cream cake with milk, eggs, cream, biscuits and fruit
chianti	dark red Tuscan wine
ciambella	ring-shaped cake
cicoria	chicory
cicorino	small chicory plants
ciliege	cherries
cime di rapa	sprouting broccoli
cioccolata	chocolate
cioccolata calda	hot chocolate
cipolle	onions
cocktail di gamberetti	shrimp cocktail
conchiglie alla marchigiana	pasta shells in tomato sauce with celery, carrot, parsley and ham
coniglio	rabbit
coniglio arrosto	roast rabbit

coniglio in umido	stewed rabbit
consommé	clear broth made with meat or chicken
contorni	vegetables
coperto	cover charge
coppa	cured neck of pork, sliced finely and eaten cold
costata alla fiorentina	T-bone veal steak
costata di manzo	beef T-bone steak
cotechino	spiced pork sausage for boiling
cotoletta	veal, pork or lamb chop
cotoletta ai ferri	grilled veal or pork chop
cotoletta alla milanese	veal chop in breadcrumbs
cotoletta alla valdostana	veal chop with ham and cheese cooked in breadcrumbs
cotolette di agnello	lamb chops
cotolette di maiale	pork chops
cozze	mussels
cozze alla marinara	mussels à la marinière
crema	custard dessert made with eggs and milk
crema al caffè	coffee custard dessert
crema al cioccolato	chocolate custard dessert
crema di funghi	cream of mushroom soup
crema di piselli	cream of pea soup
crema pasticciera	confectioner's custard
crêpe suzette	pancake flambéed with orange sauce
crescente	type of flat, fried Emilian bread made with flour, lard and eggs
crespelle	type of savoury pancake filled with white sauce and other fillings
crespelle ai funghi	savoury pancakes with mushrooms
crespelle al formaggio	savoury pancakes with cheese
crespelle al pomodoro	savoury pancakes with tomato
crostata di frutta	fruit tart
dadi	bouillon cubes
datteri	dates
degustazione	tasting
degustazione di vini	wine tasting
denominazione di origine controllata (DOC)	guarantee of quality of wine
dentice al forno	baked dentex (type of sea bream)

digestivo	digestive liqueur
dolci	sweets, desserts, cakes
endivia belga	white chicory
entrecôte (di manzo)	beef entrecote
espresso	strong black coffee
fagiano	pheasant
fagioli	beans
fagioli borlotti in umido	fresh borlotti beans (type of kidney bean) cooked in vegetables, herbs and tomato sauce
fagiolini	long, green beans
faraona	guinea fowl
fegato	liver
fegato alla veneta	liver cooked in butter with onions
fegato con salvia e burro	liver cooked in butter and sage
fettuccine	ribbon-shaped pasta
fettuccine al salmone	fettuccine with salmon
fettuccine panna e funghi	fettuccine with cream and mushrooms
fichi	figs
filetti di pesce persico	fillets of perch
filetti di sogliola	fillets of sole
filetto (di manzo)	fillet of beef
filetto ai ferri	grilled fillet of beef
filetto al cognac	fillet of beef flambé
filetto al pepe verde	fillet of beef with green peppercorns
filetto al sangue	rare fillet of beef
filetto ben cotto	well-done fillet of beef
filetto medio	medium fillet of beef
finocchio	fennel
finocchi gratinati	fennel au gratin
fonduta	cheese fondue
formaggi misti	variety of cheeses
fragole	strawberries
fragole con gelato/panna	strawberries and ice cream/cream
frappé	whisked fruit or milk drink with crushed ice
frappé al cioccolato	chocolate milk shake
frascati	dry white wine from area around Rome
frittata	type of omelette
frittata al formaggio	cheese omelette

frittata al prosciutto	ham omelette
frittata alle erbe	herb omelette
frittata alle verdure	vegetable omelette
fritto misto	mixed seafood in batter
frittura di pesce	variety of fried fish
frutta	fruit
frutta alla fiamma	fruit flambé
frutta secca	dried nuts and raisins
frutti di bosco	mixture of strawberries, raspberries, mulberries etc
frutti di mare	seafood
funghi	mushrooms
funghi trifolati	mushrooms fried in garlic and parsley
gamberetti	shrimp
gamberi	prawn
gamberoni	king prawns
gazzosa	clear lemonade
gelatina	jelly
gelato	ice cream
gelato con panna	ice cream with cream
gelato di crema	vanilla-flavoured ice cream
gelato di frutta	fruit-flavoured ice cream
gnocchetti verdi agli spinaci e al gorgonzola	small flour, potato and spinach dumplings with melted gorgonzola
gnocchi	small flour and potato dumplings
gnocchi alla romana	small milk and semolina dumplings baked with butter
gnocchi al pomodoro	small flour and potato dumplings in tomato sauce
gorgonzola	strong, soft blue cheese from Lombardy
grancevola	spiny spider crab
granchio	crab
granita	drink with crushed ice
granita di caffè	iced coffee
granita di caffè con panna	iced coffee with cream
granita di limone	lemon drink with crushed ice
grigliata di pesce	grilled fish
grigliata mista	mixed grill (meat or fish)
grissini	thin, crisp breadsticks
gruviera	Gruyère cheese

indivia	endive
insalata	salad
insalata caprese	salad of sliced tomatoes and mozzarella
insalata di funghi porcini	boletus mushroom salad
insalata di mare	seafood salad
insalata di nervetti	boiled beef or veal served cold with beans and pickles
insalata di pomodori	tomato salad
insalata di riso	rice salad
insalata mista	mixed salad
insalata russa	Russian salad
insalata verde	green salad
involtini	meat rolls stuffed with ham and herbs
lamponi	raspberries
lamponi con gelato/panna	raspberries and ice cream/cream
lasagne al forno	layers of thick, flat pasta baked in tomato sauce, mince and cheese
latte	milk
latte macchiato con cioccolato	hot, foamy milk with a sprinkling of cocoa powder
lattuga	lettuce
leggero	light
legumi	legumes
lemonsoda	sparkling lemon drink
lenticchie	lentils
lepre	hare
limonata	lemon-flavoured fizzy drink
limone	lemon
lingua	tongue
lingua salmistrata	ox tongue marinaded in brine and then cooked
macedonia di frutta	fruit salad
macedonia di frutta al maraschino	fruit salad in maraschino
macedonia di frutta con gelato	fruit salad with ice cream
maiale	pork
maionese	mayonnaise
mandarino	mandarin
mandorla	almond
manzo	beef

marroni	chestnuts
marsala	very sweet wine similar to sherry
marzapane	marzipan
mascarpone	soft, sweet cheese
medaglioni di vitello	veal medallions
mela	apple
melanzane	aubergine
melanzane alla siciliana	baked aubergine slices with parmesan, tomato sauce and egg
melone	melon
menta	mint
menu turistico	tourist menu
meringata	meringue pie
meringhe con panna	meringues with cream
merlot	dark red wine of French origin
merluzzo	cod
merluzzo alla pizzaiola	cod in tomato sauce with anchovies, capers and parsley
merluzzo in bianco	boiled cod with oil and lemon
messicani in gelatina	rolls of veal in jelly
millefoglie	layered pastry slice with confectioner's custard
minestra in brodo	noodle soup
minestrone	thick vegetable soup with rice or vermicelli
mirtilli	bilberries
mirtilli con gelato/panna	bilberries and ice cream/cream
more	mulberries or blackberries
more con gelato/panna	mulberries or blackberries and ice cream/cream
moscato	sweet, sparkling wine
mostarda di Cremona	preserve of glacé fruit in grape juice or sugar with syrup and mustard
mousse al cioccolato	chocolate mousse
mozzarella	firm, white, milky buffalo cheese
mozzarella in carrozza	slices of bread and mozzarella coated in flour and fried
nasello	hake
noce moscata	nutmeg
nocciole	hazelnuts

noci	walnuts
nodino	veal chop
olio	oil
orata al forno	baked gilthead (fish)
origano	oregano
ossobuco	stewed shin of veal
ostriche	oysters
paglia e fieno	mixture of plain and green tagliatelle
paillard di manzo	slices of grilled beef
paillard di vitello	slices of grilled veal
pane	bread
panino	filled roll
panna	cream
parmigiana di melanzane	baked dish of aubergine, tomato sauce, mozzarella and parmesan
parmigiano	parmesan cheese
pasta al forno	pasta baked in white sauce and grated cheese
pasta e fagioli	very thick soup with puréed borlotti beans and small pasta rings
pasta e piselli	pasta with peas
pasticcio di fegato d'oca	baked, pasta-covered dish with goose liver
pasticcio di lepre	baked, pasta-covered dish with hare
pasticcio di maccheroni	baked macaroni
pastina in brodo	noodle soup
patate	potatoes
patate al forno	roast potatoes
patate arrosto	roast potatoes
patate fritte	chips
patate in insalata	potato salad
pâté di carne	pâté
pâté di fegato	liver pâté
pâté di pesce	fish pâté
pecorino	strong, hard sheep's milk cheese
penne	pasta quills
penne ai quattro formaggi	pasta with sauce made from four cheeses
penne all'arrabbiata	pasta with tomato and chilli pepper sauce
penne panna e prosciutto	pasta with cream and ham sauce
pepe	pepper (spice)

peperoni	peppers
peperoni ripieni	stuffed peppers
peperoni sott'olio	peppers in oil
pera	pear
pesca	peach
pesca melba	peach melba
pesce	fish
pesce al cartoccio	fish baked in foil with herbs
pesce in carpione	marinaded fish
pinot	dry white wine from the Veneto region
pinzimonio	assorted whole, raw vegetables eaten with oil and vinegar
piselli	peas
piselli al prosciutto	fresh peas cooked in clear broth, butter, ham and basil
pizza Margherita	pizza with tomato and mozzarella
pizza Napoletana	pizza with tomato, mozzarella and anchovies
pizza quattro stagioni	pizza with tomato, mozzarella, ham, mushrooms and artichokes
pizzaiola	slices of cooked beef in tomato sauce, oregano and anchovies
pizzoccheri alla Valtellinese	thin, pasta strips with green vegetables, melted butter and cheese
polenta	yellow cornmeal boiled in water with salt, then left to set and cut in slices
polenta e funghi	polenta with mushrooms
polenta e latte	polenta with milk
polenta e osei	polenta with small birds
polenta pasticciata	alternate layers of polenta, tomato sauce and cheese
pollo	chicken
pollo alla cacciatora	chicken in white wine and mushroom sauce
pollo alla diavola	chicken pieces flattened and deep-fried
pollo al forno/arrosto	roast chicken
polpette	meatballs
polpettone	meatloaf
pomodori	tomatoes
pomodori ripieni	stuffed tomatoes

pompelmo	grapefruit
porri	leeks
prezzemolo	parsley
primi piatti	first courses
prosciutto cotto	cooked ham
prosciutto crudo	type of cured ham
prosciutto di Praga	cooked ham
prosciutto e fichi	cured ham with figs
prosciutto e melone	cured ham with melon
prugne	plums
punte di asparagi all'agro	asparagus tips in oil and lemon
purè di patate	mashed potatoes
quaglie	quails
radicchio	chicory
ragù	sauce made with mince, tomatoes and diced vegetables
rapa	type of white turnip with flavour similar to radish
rapanelli	radishes
ravioli	small, square-shaped egg pasta filled with meat or cheese
ravioli al pomodoro	ravioli stuffed with meat, in tomato sauce
razza	skate
ricotta	type of cottage cheese
risi e bisi	risotto with peas and small pieces of ham
riso	rice
riso al pomodoro	rice with tomato
riso in brodo	rice in clear broth
riso in insalata	rice salad
risotto	rice cooked in stock
risotto ai funghi	mushroom risotto
risotto al nero di seppia	black risotto made with cuttlefish ink
risotto al salmone	salmon risotto
risotto al tartufo	truffle risotto
risotto alla castellana	risotto with mushroom, ham, cream and cheese sauce
risotto alla milanese	risotto flavoured with saffron
roast-beef all'inglese	roast beef sliced very thinly and served cold with lemon
robiola	type of soft cheese from Lombardy

rognone trifolato	small kidney pieces in garlic, oil and parsley
rosatello/rosato	rosé wine
rosmarino	rosemary
salame	salami
sale	salt
salmone affumicato	smoked salmon
salsa cocktail/rosa	mayonnaise and ketchup sauce for garnishing fish and seafood
salsa di pomodoro	tomato sauce
salsa tartara	tartar sauce
salsa vellutata	white sauce made with clear broth instead of milk
salsa verde	sauce for meat made with chopped parsley and oil
salsiccia	sausage
salsiccia di cinghiale	wild boar sausage
salsiccia di maiale	pork sausage
saltimbocca alla romana	slices of veal stuffed with ham and sage and fried
salvia	sage
sambuca (con la mosca)	aniseed-flavour liqueur from Lazio region served with a coffee bean in the glass
sarde ai ferri	grilled sardines
scaloppine	veal escalopes
scaloppine ai carciofi	veal escalopes with artichokes
scaloppine ai funghi	veal escalopes with mushrooms
scaloppine al Marsala	veal escalopes in Marsala
scaloppine al prezzemolo	veal escalopes with parsley
scaloppine al vino bianco	veal escalopes in white wine
scamorza alla griglia	grilled soft cheese
scampi alla griglia	grilled scampi
secco	dry
secondi piatti	second courses, main courses
sedano	celery
selvaggina	game
semifreddo	dessert made of ice cream and sponge fingers
senape	mustard
seppie in umido	stewed cuttlefish

servizio compreso	service charge included
servizio escluso	not including service charge
soave	dry white wine from region around Lake Garda
sogliola	sole
sogliola ai ferri	grilled sole
sogliola al burro	sole cooked in butter
sogliola alla mugnaia	sole cooked in flour and butter
sorbetto	sorbet, soft ice cream
soufflé al formaggio	cheese soufflé
soufflé al prosciutto	ham soufflé
spaghetti	spaghetti
spaghetti aglio, olio e peperoncino	spaghetti with garlic, oil and crushed chilli pepper
spaghetti al pesto	spaghetti in crushed basil, garlic, oil and parmesan dressing
spaghetti al pomodoro	spaghetti in tomato sauce
spaghetti al ragù	spaghetti with meat sauce
spaghetti alla carbonara	spaghetti with egg, chopped bacon and cheese sauce
spaghetti alla puttanesca	spaghetti with anchovies, capers and black olives in tomato sauce
spaghetti alle vongole	spaghetti with clams
spaghetti all'amatriciana	spaghetti with chopped bacon and tomato sauce, typical of Rome
speck	type of cured, smoked ham
spezzatino di vitello	veal stew
spiedini	small pieces of assorted meats or fish cooked on a spit
spinaci	spinach
spinaci all'agro	spinach with oil and lemon
spremuta d'arancia	freshly squeezed orange juice
spremuta di limone	freshly squeezed lemon juice
spumante	sparkling wine
stracchino	type of soft cheese from Lombardy
stracciatella	soup of beaten eggs cooked in boiling, clear broth
strudel di mele	apple strudel
succo d'arancia	orange juice
succo di albicocca	apricot juice

succo di pera	pear juice
succo di pesca	peach juice
succo di pompelmo	grapefruit juice
sugo al tonno	tomato sauce with garlic, tuna and parsley
tacchino ripieno	stuffed turkey
tagliata	finely cut beef fillet cooked in the oven
tagliatelle	thin, flat strips of egg pasta
tagliatelle al basilico	tagliatelle and chopped basil
tagliatelle alla bolognese	tagliatelle with mince and tomato sauce
tagliatelle al pomodoro	tagliatelle with tomato sauce
tagliatelle al ragù	tagliatelle with mince and tomato sauce
tagliatelle con panna e funghi	tagliatelle with cream and mushroom sauce
tagliatelle rosse	tagliatelle with chopped red peppers
tagliatelle verdi	tagliatelle with chopped spinach
tagliolini	thin soup noodles
tagliolini ai funghi	tagliolini with mushrooms
tagliolini alla panna	tagliolini with cream
tagliolini al salmone	tagliolini with salmon
tartine	small sandwiches
tartufo	round ice cream covered in cocoa or chocolate
tè	tea
tè con latte	tea with milk
tè con limone	lemon tea
tiramisù	dessert made with coffee-soaked sponge fingers, eggs, Marsala, mascarpone and cocoa powder
tonno	tuna
torta	tart, flan
torta salata	savoury flan
torta ai carciofi	artichoke flan
torta al cioccolato	chocolate tart
torta al formaggio	cheese flan
torta di mele	apple tart
torta di noci	walnut tart
torta di ricotta	type of cheesecake
torta di zucchine	courgette flan
torta gelato	ice-cream tart
tortellini	small pasta shapes filled with minced pork, ham, parmesan and nutmeg

tortellini alla panna	tortellini with cream
tortellini al pomodoro	tortellini with tomato sauce
tortellini al ragù	tortellini with mince and tomato sauce
tortellini in brodo	tortellini in clear broth
tortelloni di magro/di ricotta	pasta shapes filled with cheese, parsley and chopped vegetables
tortelloni di zucca	tortelloni stuffed with pumpkin
trancio di palombo	smooth dogfish steak
trancio di pesce spada	swordfish steak
trenette col pesto	type of flat spaghetti with crushed basil, garlic, oil and cheese sauce
triglie	mullet (fish)
trippa	tripe
trota	trout
trota affumicata	smoked trout
trota al burro	trout cooked in butter
trota alle mandorle	trout with almonds
trota bollita	boiled trout
uccelletti	small birds wrapped in bacon, served on cocktail sticks
uova	eggs
uova al tegamino con pancetta	fried eggs and bacon
uova alla coque	boiled eggs
uova farcite	eggs with tuna, capers and mayonnaise filling
uova sode	hard-boiled eggs
uva	grapes
uva bianca	white grapes
uva nera	black grapes
vellutata di asparagi	creamed asparagus with egg yolks
vellutata di piselli	creamed peas with egg yolks
verdura	vegetables
vermicelli	very fine, thin pasta, often used in soups
vino	wine
vino bianco	white wine
vino da dessert	dessert wine
vino da pasto	table wine
vino da tavola	table wine
vino rosso	red wine
vitello	veal

vitello tonnato	cold sliced veal in tuna, anchovy, oil and lemon sauce
vongole	clams
würstel	hot dog
zabaione	creamy dessert made from beaten eggs, sugar and Marsala
zafferano	saffron
zucca	pumpkin
zucchine	courgette
zucchine al pomodoro	chopped courgette in tomato, garlic and parsley sauce
zucchine ripiene	stuffed courgette
zuccotto	ice-cream cake with sponge fingers, cream and chocolate
zuppa	soup
zuppa di cipolle	onion soup
zuppa di cozze	mussel soup
zuppa di lenticchie	lentil soup
zuppa di pesce	fish soup
zuppa di verdura	vegetable soup
zuppa inglese	trifle

SHOPS AND SERVICES

This chapter covers all kinds of shopping needs and services.
To start with you'll find some general phrases that can be used
in lots of different places – many of these are listed below.
After the general phrases come more specific requests and
sentences to use when you've found what you need, be it food,
clothing, repairs, film-developing, a haircut or bargaining in
the market. Don't forget to refer to the mini-dictionary for
items you may be looking for.

Shops are usually open from 8.30 or 9 am to 12.30 or 1 pm
and from 3.30 or 4 pm to 7.30 or 8 pm, and often later in
tourist resorts in peak season. Shopping hours may vary
slightly according to the region you are in, and shops may
close on different days of the week – often on Monday
mornings, all day Monday, or on Thursday afternoons. Venice
has half-day closing (only in winter) on Monday mornings. In
Florence, stores are closed on Monday mornings or all day
Monday in the winter, autumn, and spring, and are closed on
Saturday afternoons in August. Most large shops and
supermarkets are open Monday to Saturday.

It's acceptable to bargain in the market, but only if the price
is not displayed.

In Italy, **chili** (kilos) and **etti** (hectograms) are used.
One **etto** = 100 grams. Cheese, ham etc are generally sold by
the **etto** and fruit and vegetables by the **chili**.

Chemists are very expensive in Italy (see Health, page 113).
If you should need items such as antiseptic cream, toothpaste,
plasters, tampons etc, it's better to go to a supermarket or a
drogheria (*drogairee-a*), which is like a chemist and general
grocery combined. If you wish to buy perfume or
sophisticated cosmetic products, you should go to a **profumeria**
(*profoomairee-a*). If you want to buy film or get your photos
developed, go to a photographic shop or an optician's, not to a
chemist.

In Italy you won't find the type of laundrette where you can do your own washing and drying. A dry cleaner's will only accept clothes for dry cleaning or large items such as bed linen, but not small personal items.

For cigarettes, stamps, chewing gum and postcards, go to a **tabaccaio**, which can be identified by a sign with a white **T** on a black background. A **tabaccaio** generally has the same opening hours as shops. After 8 pm, you can only buy cigarettes in specially licensed bars or in railway stations.

Useful Words and Phrases

antique shop	il negozio di antiquariato	*negotz-yo dee anteekwar-yato*
audio equipment shop	il negozio di hi-fi	*negotz-yo dee 'hi-fi'*
bakery	la panetteria	*panet-tairee-a*
bookshop	la libreria	*leebrairee-a*
butcher's shop	la macelleria	*machel-lairee-a*
buy	comprare	*komprare*
cake shop	la pasticceria	*pasteechairee-a*
camera store	il negozio di macchine fotografiche	*negotz-yo dee mak-keene fotografeeke*
camping equipment	l'attrezzatura da campeggio	*at-tretz-zatoora da kampej-jo*
cash register	la cassa	*kas-sa*
cheap	economico	*ekonomeeko*
chemist	la farmacia	*farmachee-a*
china	la porcellana	*porchel-lana*
cost	prezzo	*pretzo*
craft store	il negozio di artigianato	*negotz-yo dee arteejanato*
department store	il grande magazzino	*grande magatzeeno*
(large)	l'ipermecato	*eepairmairkato*

dry cleaner's	la lavanderia a secco,	*lavandairee-a a sek-ko,*
	la tintoria	*teentoree-a*
electrical goods shop	il negozio di articoli elettrici	*negotz-yo dee arteekolee elet-treechee*
expensive	caro, costoso	*karo, kostozo*
fishmonger's	la pescheria	*peskairee-a*
florist's	fioraio	*f-yora-yo*
fruit	la frutta	*froot-ta*
gift shop	il negozio di articoli da regalo	*negotz-yo dee arteekolee da regalo*
grocer's	l'alimentari	*aleementaree*
hairdresser's		
(men's)	barbiere	*barb-yaire*
(women's)	parrucchiere, acconciature	*par-rookk-yaire, ak-konchatoore*
hardware shop	il ferramenta	*fair-ramenta*
indoor market	il mercato coperto	*mairkato kopairto*
jeweller's	la gioielleria	*joyel-lairee-a*
market	il mercato	*mairkato*
menswear	l'abbigliamento da uomo	*ab-beel-yamento da womo*
newsagent's	l'edicola	*edeecola*
optician's	il ottico	*ot-teeko*
produce market	il negozio di frutta e verdura	*negotz-yo dee froot-ta ay verdoora*
receipt	lo scontrino	*skontreeno*
record shop	il negozio di dischi	*negotz-yo dee deeskee*
sale	la svendita, i saldi	*zvendeeta, saldee*
shoe repairer's	il calzolaio	*kaltzola-yo*
shoe shop	il negozio di scarpe	*negotz-yo dee skarpe*
shop	il negozio	*negotz-yo*
shopping bag	il sacchetto	*sak-ket-to*
souvenir shop	il negozio di souvenir	*negotz-yo dee sooveneer*

sports equipment	l'attrezzatura sportiva	*at-tretz-zatoora sporteeva*
sportswear	l'abbigliamento sportivo	*ab-beel-yamento sporteevo*
stationer's	la cartoleria	*kartolairee-a*
supermarket	il supermercato	*soopairmairkato*
sweet shop	la pasticceria	*pasteech-chairee-a*
tailor	il sarto	*sarto*
tobacconist's	il tabaccaio	*tabak-ka-yo*
toy shop	il negozio di giocattoli	*negotz-yo dee jokat-tolee*
travel agent	l'agenzia di viaggio	*ajentzee-a dee vee-aj-jo*
vegetables	la verdura	*vairdoora*
wine merchant	la enoteca	*enotaika*
women's wear	l'abbigliamento per signora	*ab-beel-yamento pair seen-yora*

Excuse me, where is/where are …?
Mi scusi, dov'è/dove sono …?
mee skoozee doveh/dove sono

Where is there a … (shop)?
Dov'è un negozio di … qui vicino?
doveh oon negotz-yo dee … kwee veecheeno

Where is the … department?
Dov'è il reparto …?
doveh eel reparto

Where is the main shopping area?
Dov'è la zona dei negozi?
doveh la zona day negotzi

Is there a market here?
C'è un mercato qui?
cheh oon mairkato kwee

I'd like …
Vorrei …
vor-ray

Do you have …?
Avete …?
avete

How much is this?
Quanto costa questo?
kwanto kosta kwesto

Where do I pay?
Dove si paga?
dove see paga

Do you take credit cards?
Accettate carte di credito?
ach-chet-tate karte dee kredeeto

I think perhaps you've short-changed me
Penso che abbiate sbagliato nel darmi il resto
penso ke abb-yate sbal-yato nel darmee eel resto

Can I have a receipt/a bag, please?
Potrebbe darmi lo scontrino/un sacchetto?
potreb-be darmee lo skontreeno/oon sak-ket-to

I'm just looking
Sto solo dando un'occhiata
sto solo dando oon okk-yata

I'll come back later
Tornerò più tardi
tornairo p-yoo tardee

Do you have any more of these?
Ne ha ancora di questi?
ne a ankora dee kwestee

Have you anything cheaper?
Non ha niente di più economico?
non a n-yente dee p-yoo ekonomeeko

Have you anything larger/smaller?
Non ne ha uno più grande/piccolo?
non ne a oono p-yoo grande/peek-kolo

Can I try it/them on?
Posso provarlo/provarli?
pos-so provarlo/provarlee

Does it come in other colours?
C'è anche in altri colori?
cheh anke een altree koloree

Could you gift wrap it for me?
Può farmi un pacchetto regalo?
pwo farmee oon pak-ket-to regalo

I'd like to exchange this; it's defective
Vorrei cambiare questo: è difettoso
vor-ray kamb-yare kwesto: eh deefet-tozo

I'm afraid I don't have the receipt
Mi dispiace, ma non ho lo scontrino
mee deesp-yache ma non o lo skontreeno

Can I have a refund?
Posso riavere indietro i soldi?
pos-so ree-avaire endee-etro ee soldee

My camera isn't working
La mia macchina fotografica non funziona
la mee-a mak-keena fotografeeka non foontz-yona

I want a roll of 36-exposure colour film, 100 ISO
Vorrei una pellicola 100ISO a colori da 36 foto
vor-ray oona pel-leekola 100 ee-esse-o a koloree da 36 foto

I'd like this film processed
Vorrei sviluppare questa pellicola
vor-ray sveeloop-pare kwesta pel-leekola

Matte/glossy prints
Fotografie su carta opaca/lucida
fotografee-e soo karta opaka/loocheeda

One-hour service, please
Vorrei il servizio in un'ora, per favore
vor-ray eel serveetz-yo een oon ora pair favore

Where can I get this repaired?
Dove posso farlo riparare?
dove pos-so farlo reeparare

Can you repair this?
Può aggiustarmelo?
pwo aj-joostarmelo

I'd like this skirt/these trousers dry-cleaned
Vorrei far lavare a secco questa gonna/questi pantaloni
vor-ray far lavarai a sec-co kwesta gon-na/kwestee pantalonee

When will it/they be ready?
Quando sarà pronto/saranno pronti?
kwando sara pronto/saran-no prontee

I'd like to make an appointment
Vorrei prendere un appuntamento
vor-ray prendaire oon ap-poontamento

I want a cut and blow-dry
Vorrei taglio e messa in piega (con il föhn)
vor-ray tal-yo ay mes-sa een p-yega kon eel fon

With conditioner/No conditioner, thanks
Con il balsamo/Senza il balsamo, grazie
kon eel bal-samo/sentza eel bal-samo gratzee-e

Just a trim, please
Solo una spuntatina, per favore
solo oona spoontateena pair favore

Not too much off!
Non tagli troppo!
non tal-yee trop-po

When does the market open?
Quando apre il mercato?
kwando apre eel mairkato

What's the price per kilo?
Quanto costa al chilo?
kwanto kosta al keelo

Could you write that down?
Può scriverlo?
pwo skreevairlo

That's too much! I'll pay …
È troppo! Le do …
eh trop-po! le do

Could I have a discount?
Potrebbe farmi uno sconto?
potreb-be farmee oono skonto

That's fine. I'll take it!
Va bene. Lo prendo!
va bene. lo prendo

I'll have a piece of that cheese
Vorrei un pezzo di quel formaggio
vor-ray oon petz-zo dee kwel formaj-jo

About 250/500 grams
Circa duecentocinquanta/cinquecento grammi
cheerka doo-e-chentocheenkwanta/cheenkwechento gram-mee

A kilo/half a kilo of apples, please
Un chilo/mezzo chilo di mele, per favore
oon keelo/metzo keelo dee mele pair favore

250 grams of that cheese, please
Due etti e mezzo di quel formaggio, per favore
doo-e et-tee ay metzo dee kwel formaj-jo pair favore

May I taste it?
Posso assaggiarlo?
pos-so as-saj-jarlo

That's very nice, I'll take some
Quello è molto buono; ne prenderò un po'
kwel-lo eh molto bwono; ne prendairo oon po

It isn't what I wanted
Non è quello che volevo
non eh kwel-lo ke volevo

THINGS YOU'LL SEE

abbigliamento da uomo	men's clothing
abbigliamento per signora	women's clothing
acconciature	women's hairdresser
agenzia di viaggio	travel agency
alimentari	grocer's
barbiere	barber's
calzature	shoes
cartoleria	stationer's
cassa	cashier, cash register
coiffeur	hairdresser
colpi di sole	highlights
dolci	confectionery, cakes
dozzina	dozen
elettrodomestici	electrical appliances
entrata	entrance

→

fai-da-te	hardware shop
fioraio	florist
forniture per ufficio	office supplies
fresco	fresh
giocattoli	toys
grande magazzino	department store
la merce venduta non si cambia senza lo scontrino	goods are not exchanged without a receipt
libreria	bookshop
liquori	liquor
macelleria	butcher's shop
messa in piega con il föhn	blow-dry
moda	fashion
munitevi di un carrello/cestino	please take a trolley/basket
pagare alla cassa	pay at the desk
panetteria	bakery
parrucchiere (per signora)	women's hairdresser
pasticceria	cake shop
pellicceria	furrier
permanente	perm
pescheria	fishmonger's
piano superiore	upper floor
prezzo	price
prima qualità	high quality
reparto	department
ridotto	reduced
riviste	magazines
saldi	sales
sartoria	tailor's
spingere	push
spuntata	trim
svendita	sale
tabacchi	tobacco
taglio	cut

→

tirare	pull
uscita	exit
verdure	vegetables

THINGS YOU'LL HEAR

Desidera?
Can I help you?

La stanno servendo?
Are you being served?

Non ha spiccioli?
Haven't you anything smaller? (money)

Mi dispiace quest'articolo è esaurito
I'm sorry, we're out of stock

Questo è tutto quello che abbiamo
This is all we have

Ha spiccioli/moneta?
Do you have any change?

Diamo solamente buoni acquisto
We only give credit notes

Si accomodi alla cassa, prego
Please pay at the till

Nient'altro?
Will there be anything else?

Quanto ne vuole?
How much would you like?

Come lo desidera?
How would you like it?

SPORT

Whether you enjoy sport as a passive spectator or as an active participant, Italy has a great deal to offer. The Italians are passionate football fans, and the championships are played from September to May, with international matches throughout the year. Cycling is also a favourite Italian sport, and the **Giro d'Italia** – the annual race around the peninsula – takes place during May and June.

Summer sports include fishing, golf, skin diving, swimming and tennis. There is no lack of fine beaches in Italy, and most of them are well-managed and provide everything for the tourist's enjoyment. There are numerous windsurfing schools where you can take lessons and hire all the necessary equipment, from boards to wet suits. One of the most notable areas for this sport is Lake Garda.

Italy is a haven for mountain climbers and hikers, who will delight in discovering the many beautiful Alpine and Apennine valleys unknown to the average tourist. For winter sports there are excellently equipped skiing resorts in the Dolomites and in the Piedmont and Lombardy regions of Northern Italy.

USEFUL WORDS AND PHRASES

athletics	l'atletica	*atleteeka*
ball	la palla	*pal-la*

**beginners'
  slope**
	la pista per
	   principianti
		*peesta pair
		   preencheep-yantee*

bicycle	la bicicletta	*beecheeklet-ta*
binding (*ski*)	l'attacco (degli sci)	*at-tak-ko del-yee shee*
cable car	la funivia	*fooneevee-a*
canoe/canoeing	la canoa	*kano-a*
chairlift	la seggiovia	*sej-jovee-a*
cycling	il ciclismo	*cheekleezmo*

go cycling	andare in
	   bicicletta
		*andare een
		   beecheeklet-ta*

cross-country skiing	lo sci di fondo	*shee dee fondo*
dive	tuffarsi	*toof-farsee*
diving board	il trampolino	*trampoleeno*
downhill skiing	lo sci da discesa	*shee da deesheza*
fishing	la pesca	*peska*
fishing rod	la canna da pesca	*kan-na da peska*
flippers	le pinne	*peen-ne*
football	il calcio	*kalcho*
(ball)	il pallone	*pal-lone*
football match	la partita di calcio	*parteeta dee kalcho*
game *(match)*	la partita	*parteeta*
goggles	gli occhialetti	*ok-kyalet-ti*
golf course	il campo da golf	*kampo da 'golf'*
play golf	giocare a golf	*jokare a 'golf'*
gymnastics	la ginnastica	*jeen-nasteeka*
hang gliding	il deltaplano	*deltaplano*
harpoon	l'arpione	*arp-yone*
hunting	la caccia	*kach-cha*
ice hockey	l'hockey su ghiaccio	*'hockey' soo g-yach-cho*
mask	la maschera	*maskaira*
mast	l'albero	*albairo*
mountaineering	l'alpinismo	*alpeeneezmo*
oxygen bottles	le bombole di ossingeno	*bombolay dee os-seejeno*
parasailing	il parapendio	*parapendee-o*
pedal boat	il pedalò	*pedalo*
race track	la pista	*peesta*
racket	la racchetta	*rak-ket-ta*
ride	andare a cavallo	*andare a kaval-lo*
riding	l'equitazione	*ekweetatz-yone*
riding hat	il cappello da fantino	*kap-pel-lo da fanteeno*
rock climbing	l'alpinismo	*alpeeneezmo*
saddle	la sella	*sel-la*
sail	la vela	*vela*
sailboard	il surf	*'surf'*
sailing	andare a vela	*andare a vela*

shooting range	il tiro a segno	*teero a sen-yo*
skate	pattinare	*pat-teenare*
skates	i pattini	*pat-teenee*
skating rink	la pista di pattinaggio	*peesta dee pateenaj-jo*
ski (*verb*)	sciare	*shee-are*
ski boots	gli scarponi da sci	*skarponee da shee*
skiing	lo sci	*shee*
skin diving	l'immersione subacquea	*eem-mairsyone soobakwe-a*
ski pass	lo ski pass	*'ski pass'*
ski poles	i bastoncini	*bastoncheenee*
skis	gli sci	*shee*
ski tow	lo skilift	*'skilift'*
ski trail	la pista da sci	*peesta da shee*
ski wax	la sciolina	*shee-oleena*
sled	la slitta	*zleeta*
snorkel	boccaglio	*bok-kalyo*
sports centre	il centro sportivo	*chentro sporteevo*
stadium	lo stadio	*stad-yo*
surfboard	il surf	*'surf'*
swim	nuotare	*nwotare*
swimming pool	la piscina	*peesheena*
team	la squadra	*skwadra*
tennis court	il campo da tennis	*kampo da ten-nis*
toboggan	la slitta	*zleeta*
underwater fishing	la pesca subacquea	*peska soobakwe-a*
volleyball	pallavolo	*pal-lavolo*
water-ski	fare sci d'acqua	*fare shee dakwa*
water-skiing	lo sci d'acqua	*shee dakwa*
water-skis	gli sci d'acqua	*shee dakwa*
wet suit	la muta da sub	*moota da soob*
go windsurfing	praticare il windsurf	*prateekare eel 'windsurf'*

How do I get to the beach?
Potrebbe indicarmi la strada per la spiaggia?
potreb-be eendeekarmee la strada pair la sp-yaj-ja

How deep is the water here?
Quant'è profonda qui l'acqua?
kwanteh profonda kwee lakwa

Is there an indoor/outdoor pool here?
C'è una piscina coperta/scoperta?
cheh oona peesheena kopairta/skopairta

Is it dangerous to swim here?
È pericoloso nuotare qui?
eh paireekolozo nwotare kwee

Can I fish here?
Posso pescare qui?
pos-so peskare kwee

Do I need a licence?
C'è bisogno della licenza?
cheh beezon-yo del-la leechentza

Is there a golf course near here?
C'è un campo da golf da queste parti?
cheh oon kampo da 'golf' da kweste partee

Do I have to be a member?
È necessario essere socio?
eh neches-sar-yo es-saire socho

Where can I hire …?
Dove posso noleggiare …?
dove pos-so nolej-jare

I would like to hire a bike/some skis
Vorrei noleggiare una bicicletta/degli sci
vor-ray nolej-jare oona beecheeklet-ta/del-yee shee

How much does it cost per hour/day?
Quanto costa all'ora/al giorno?
kwanto kosta al ora/al jorno

When does the lift start?
A che ora aprono gli impianti?
a ke ora aprono l-yee eemp-yantee

What are the snow conditions like today?
Quali sono le condizioni della neve oggi?
kwalee sono le kondeetz-yonee del-la neve oj-jee

How much is a daily/weekly lift pass?
Quanto costa un abbonamento giornaliero/settimanale?
kwanto kosta oon ab-bonamento jornal-yairo/set-tee-manale

I would like to take skiing lessons
Vorrei prendere lezioni di sci
vor-ray prendaire letz-yonee dee shee

Where are the nursery slopes?
Dove sono le discese per principianti?
dove sono le deesheze pair preencheep-yantee

Is it very steep?
È molto ripido?
eh molto reepeedo

I would like to take water-skiing lessons
Vorrei prendere lezioni di sci d'acqua
vor-ray prendaire letz-yonee dee shee dakwa

There's something wrong with this binding
C'è qualcosa che non va in questo attacco
cheh kwalkoza ke non va een kwesto at-tak-ko

I haven't played this before
Non ho mai provato prima
non o mi provato preema

Let's go skating/swimming
Andiamo a pattinare/sciare
and-yamo a pat-teenare/shee-are

What's the score?
A quanto sono?
a kwanto sono

Who won?
Chi ha vinto?
kee a veento

THINGS YOU'LL SEE

alla seggiovia	to the chairlift
correnti pericolose	dangerous currents
divieto di balneazione	no bathing
divieto di pesca	no fishing
funivia	cable car
noleggio barche	boat hire
noleggio biciclette	bicycle hire
noleggio sci	ski hire
non dondolarsi	no swinging
pedoni	pedestrians
pericolo	danger
pericolo di valanghe	danger of avalanches
piscina coperta	indoor swimming pool
piscina scoperta	outdoor swimming pool
pista ciclabile	cycle path
pista da fondo	cross-country ski track
pista facile/difficile	easy/difficult slope
pista per slitte	toboggan run
prepararsi a scendere	get ready to alight
pronto soccorso	first aid
sci di fondo	cross-country skiing
scuola di sci	ski school
trampolino	diving board; ski jump
vietato bagnarsi	no bathing
vietato pescare	no fishing
vietato tuffarsi	no diving

POST OFFICES AND BANKS

Main post offices are open from 8.15 am to 7 pm, while local offices generally close at 2 pm. Postboxes in Italy are usually red, although there are some yellow ones. Stamps can be bought at the post office or, more conveniently, at any **tabaccaio** (tobacconist's). These are easily identified by the sign displayed outside – a white **T** on a black background.

Banks are open from 8.30 am to 1.30 pm and from 2.45 pm to 3.45 pm, from Monday to Friday. Generally speaking, it is better to change money in a bank than in an exchange office (called **cambio** or **cambiavalute**), because the latter charges a commission. Exchange offices are found in airports, stations, and in the city centre. In larger cities, you will find automatic exchange offices with cash machines outside some banks.

You will find cash machines for bank and credit cards outside the main banks (but a commission of about five percent is charged if you draw money with a credit card). Major credit cards are generally accepted in hotels, restaurants and shops. Small shops or restaurants do not accept them.

The Italian unit of currency is the common European currency, the **euro** (*ayoo-ro*). One **euro** is divided into 100 **centesimi** (*chen-teseemee*), and the coins come in 1, 2, 5, 10, 20 and 50 **centesimi**; 1 and 2 **euros**. Notes are available in 5, 10, 20, 50, 100, 200 and 500 **euros**.

Useful Words and Phrases

airmail	la posta aerea	*posta a-aire-a*
bank	la banca	*banka*
banknote	la banconota	*bankonota*
cash (*noun*)	il denaro	*denaro*
cash machine	lo sportello automatico	*sportel-lo owtomateeko*
change (*verb*)	cambiare	*kamb-yare*
cheque	l'assegno	*as-sen-yo*

chequebook	il libretto degli assegni	*leebret-to del-yee as-sen-yee*
collection	la levata	*levata*
counter	lo sportello	*sportel-lo*
credit card	la carta di credito	*karta dee kredeeto*
customs form	il modulo per la dogana	*modoolo pair la dogana*
delivery	la consegna	*konsen-ya*
deposit *(noun)*	il deposito	*depozeeto*
(verb)	depositare	*depozeetare*
envelope	la busta	*boosta*
exchange rate	il tasso di cambio	*tas-so dee kam-bee-o*
fax *(noun)*	il fax	*'fax'*
(verb)	spedire via fax	*spedeere vee-a 'fax'*
fax machine	il fax	*'fax'*
form	il modulo	*modoolo*
international money order	il vaglia postale internazionale	*val-ja postale eentairnatz-yonale*
letter	la lettera	*let-taira*
money order	il vaglia postale	*val-ya postale*
package/parcel	il pacchetto, il pacco	*pak-ket-to, pak-ko*
post *(noun)*	la posta	*posta*
(verb)	spedire	*spedeere*
postage rates	le tariffe postali	*tareef-fe postalee*
postal order	il vaglia postale	*val-ya postale*
post box	la cassetta delle lettere	*cas-set-ta del-le let-taire*
postcard	la cartolina	*kartoleena*
post code	il codice di avviamento postale	*kodeeche dee avv-yamento postale*
poste restante	fermo posta	*fairmo posta*
postman	il postino	*posteeno*
post office	l'ufficio postale	*oof-feecho postale*
registered letter	la raccomandata	*rak-komandata*
stamp	il francobollo	*frankobol-lo*

surface mail	la posta ordinaria	*posta ordeengree-a*
telegram	il telegramma	*telegram-ma*
traveller's cheque	il traveller's cheque	*'traveller's cheque'*
withdraw	prelevare	*prelevare*

How much is a postcard to …?
Quanto costa spedire una cartolina in …?
kwanto kosta spedeere oona kartoleena een

I would like three 60-cent stamps
Vorrei tre francobolli da settanta centesimi
vor-ray tre frankobol-lee da set-tanta chen-teseemee

I want to register this letter
Vorrei spedire questa lettera per raccomandata
vor-ray spedeere kwesta let-taira pair rak-komandata

I want to send this package to …
Vorrei spedire questo pacco in …
vor-ray spedeere kwesto pak-ko een

How long does the post to … take?
Quanto ci mette la posta per arrivare in …?
kwanto chee met-te la posta pair ar-reevare een

Where can I post this?
Dove posso imbucarlo?
dove pos-so eembookarlo

Is there any post for me?
C'è posta per me?
cheh posta pair me

I'd like to send a fax
Vorrei spedire un fax
vor-ray spedeere oon fax

This is to go airmail
Deve essere spedito per via aerea
deve es-saire spedeeto pair vee-a a-aire-a

I'd like to change this into 10 euro notes
Vorrei cambiare in banconote da dieci euro
vor-ray kamb-yare een bankonote da dee-echee ayoo-ro

Can I cash these traveller's cheques?
Posso cambiare questi traveller's cheques?
pos-so kamb-yare kwestee 'traveller's cheques'

What is the exchange rate for the pound?
Qual è il tasso di cambio della sterlina?
kwaleh eel tas-so dee kam-bee-o del-la stairleena

Can I draw cash using this credit card?
Posso fare un prelievo usando la carta di credito?
pos-so fare oon prel-yevo oozando la karta dee kredeeto

I'd like it in 20 euro notes
Vorrei banconote da venti euro
vor-ray bankonote da ventee ayoo-ro

Could you give me smaller notes?
Può darmi banconote di piccolo taglio?
pwo darmee bankonote dee peek-kolo tal-yo

THINGS YOU'LL SEE

affrancatura	postage
affrancatura per l'estero	postage abroad
assicurata	insured mail
cambiavalute/cambio	bureau de change
cartolina	postcard
codice (di avviamento) postale	post code
compilare	to fill in
conto corrente	current account
deposito	deposit
destinatario	addressee

→

espresso	express
fermo posta	poste restante
francobollo	stamp
indirizzo	address
lettera	letter
orario di apertura	opening hours
mittente	sender
pacchetto	package
posta	mail
posta aerea	airmail
prelievo	withdrawal
raccomandata	registered letter
riempire	to fill in
sportello	counter
sportello pacchi	packages counter
tariffa	rate, charge
tariffa interna	domestic postage

COMMUNICATIONS

Telephones: Old telephone boxes can be operated with **gettoni** – tokens – but they are being replaced with newer phones which take phonecards. These cost 1, 2.5, 5, or 8 euros and can be bought at tobacconists'. You need to snap off the corner of the card to start using it.

If you want to make a long-distance phone call, it is better to go to an office of the Italian national telephone company, the **Telecom Italia**, which is a department of the main post office in Florence and Venice. Or, you can ask in a bar if they have **un telefono a scatti** – you make your call first and are then charged for the number of units you have used. To call the UK, dial 0044 then the number (omit the first zero of the area code).

The tones you'll hear when telephoning in Italy are:

Dialling tone: two tones, one short and one long, at
                 regular intervals;
Ringing tone: one single, long tone at regular intervals;
Engaged tone: short rapid beeps.

USEFUL WORDS AND PHRASES

answering machine	la segretaria telefonica	*segretareea telefoneeka*
call *(noun)*	la telefonata	*telefonata*
(verb)	telefonare	*telefonare*
cardphone	il telefono a scheda	*telefono a skeda*
code	il prefisso	*prefees-so*
crossed line	l'interferenza	*eentairfairentza*
dial	fare il numero	*fare eel noomairo*
dialling tone	il segnale di libero	*sen-yale dee leebairo*
directory enquiries	il servizio informazioni telefoniche	*sairveetz-yo eenformatz-yonee telefoneeke*
email	la posta elettronica	*posta ai-lait-tronee-ka*

101

emergency	l'emergenza	*emairjentza*
extension	l'interno	*eentairno*
fax machine	il fax	*'fax'*
international call	la chiamata internazionale	*k-yamata eentairnatz-yonale*
internet	l'internet	*'internet'*
mobile phone	il telefonino	*telefonino*
modem	il modem	*'modem'*
number	il numero	*noomairo*
operator	l'operatore	*opairatore*
payphone	il telefono a gettoni	*telefono a jet-tonee*
phonecard	la scheda telefonica	*skeda telefoneeka*
photocopier	la fotcopiatrice	*fotokopee-atreece*
receiver	il ricevitore	*reecheveetore*
reverse charge call	la chiamata a carico del destinatario	*k-yamata a kareeko del desteenataree-o*
telephone	il telefono	*telefono*
telephone box	la cabina telefonica	*kabeena telefoneeka*
Web site	il sito internet	*seeto 'internet'*
wrong number	il numero sbagliato	*noomairo zbal-yato*

Where is the nearest telephone box?
Dov'è la cabina telefonica più vicina?
doveh la kabeena telefoneeka p-yoo veecheena

Is there a telephone directory?
C'è una guida telefonica?
cheh oona gweeda telefoneeka

Can I call abroad from here?
Posso fare una telefonata internazionale da qua?
pos-so fare oona telefonata eentairnatz-yonale da kwa

I would like to make a reverse charge call
La metta a carico del destinatario
la met-ta a kareeko del desteenataree-o

I would like a number in …
Ho bisogno del numero di un abbonato di …
o beezon-yo del noomairo dee oon ab-bonato dee

How do I get an outside line?
Come devo fare per avere una linea esterna?
kome devo fare pair avaire oona leene-a estairna

Hello, this is … speaking
Pronto, sono …
pronto sono

Is that …?
Parlo con …?
parlo kon

Speaking
Sono io/pronto
sono ee-o/pronto

I would like to speak to …
Vorrei parlare con …
vor-ray parlare kon

Extension …, please
Interno …, per favore
eentairno … pair favore

Please tell him/her … called
Per cortesia, gli/le dica che ha telefonato …
pair kortezee-a l-yee/le deeka ke a telefonato

Ask him/her to call me back, please
Mi fa richiamare, per favore
mee fa reekeeamare, pair favore

My number is …
Il mio numero è …
eel mee-o noomairo eh

Do you know where he/she is?
Non sa dov'è?
non sa doveh

When will he/she be back?
Quando tornerà?
kwando tornaira

Could you leave him/her a message?
Potrebbe lasciargli/lasciarle un messaggio?
potreb-be lasharl-yee/lasharle oon mes-saj-jo

I'll call back later
Richiamero più tardi
reekeeah-mayro p-yoo tardee

Sorry, I've got the wrong number
Mi scusi, ho sbagliato numero
mee skoozee oh zbal-yato noomairo

What's your fax number/email address?
Qual'è il suo numero di fax/posta elettronica?
kwal-ai eel soo-o noo-mairo dee fax/posta ai-lait-tronee-ka

Did you get my fax/email?
Ha/hai ricevuto il mio fax/la mia posta elettronica?
a/aee ree-ceh-voo-to eel mee-o fax/posta ai-lait-tronee-ka

Please resend your fax
Mi rimanda il suo/mi rimandi il tuo fax, per favore
mee ree-manda eel soo-o/mee ree-mandee eel too-o fax, pair favore

Can I send an email/fax from here?
Posso inviare della posta elettronica/un fax da qui?
pos-so eenvee-arai del-la posta ai-lait-tronee-ka/oon fax da kwee

Can I use the photocopier/fax machine?
Posso usare la fotocopiatrice/il fax?
pos-so oosarai la fotokopee-atreece/eel fax

THE ALPHABET

a	*ah*	h	*ak-ka*	o	*o*	v	*voo*
b	*bee*	i	*ee*	p	*pee*	w	*voo dopp-yo*
c	*chee*	j	*ee-loonga*	q	*koo*	x	*eeks*
d	*dee*	k	*kap-pa*	r	*air-e*	y	*eepseelon*
e	*ay*	l	*el-le*	s	*es-se*	z	*tse-ta*
f	*ef-fe*	m	*em-me*	t	*tee*		
g	*jee*	n	*en-ne*	u	*oo*		

THINGS YOU'LL SEE

apparecchio	phone
centralino	local exchange, operator
chiamata	call
chiamata in teleselezione	direct dialling
chiamata interurbana	long-distance call
chiamata urbana	local call
fuori servizio	out of order
gettoni	telephone tokens
guida telefonica	telephone directory
il servizio è gratuito	free service
indirizzo di posta elettronica	email address
inserire le monete	insert coins
moneta	coin
numeri utili	useful numbers
Pagine Gialle	Yellow Pages
prefissi telefonici	area codes
riagganciare	hang up
ricevitore	receiver
scatto	unit
selezionare il numero	dial the number
servizio guasti	faulty service
sollevare	to lift
telefonino	mobile phone

THINGS YOU'LL HEAR

Pronto
Hello

Sono io/pronto
Speaking

Con chi vuole parlare?
Who would you like to speak to?

Ha sbagliato numero
You've got the wrong number

Chi parla?
Who's calling?

Attenda in linea, prego
Hold, please

Mi dispiace, non c'è
I'm sorry, he/she's not in

Posso richiamarla?
Can I call you back?

Che numero ha?
What is your number?

Tornerà alle …
He/she'll be back at … o'clock

Richiami domani, per favore
Please call again tomorrow

Gli dirò che ha chiamato
I'll tell him you called

EMERGENCIES

Information on local health services can be obtained from
tourist information offices, but in an emergency dial 113,
which is a general emergency number. Dial 115 for the fire
department and 118 for an ambulance.

Remember that there is more than one type of police force in
Italy: **carabinieri** are a military force and **polizia** are a civil
force dealing with crime. In case of emergency, dial either 113
for **polizia** or 112 for **carabinieri**.

For emergency breakdown services, dial 116 (or 01 in the
provinces of Potenza, Catanzaro, Lecce or Caltanisetta). You
will be put in touch with the **ACI** (Italian Automobile Club),
which will provide immediate assistance. (Also see Driving,
page 37.)

USEFUL WORDS AND PHRASES

accident	l'incidente	*eencheedente*
ambulance	l'ambulanza	*amboolantza*
assault	aggredire	*ag-gredeere*
breakdown	il guasto	*gwasto*
break down *(verb)*	guastarsi	*gwastarsee*
burglar	il ladro	*ladro*
burglary	il furto	*foorto*
casualty	il pronto soccorso	*pronto so-korso*
crash *(noun)*	l'incidente	*eencheedente*
(verb)	avere un	*avaire oon*
	incidente	*eencheedente*
emergency	l'emergenza	*emairjentza*
fire *(flames)*	il fuoco	*fwoko*
(event)	l'incendio	*eenchend-yo*
fire brigade	i vigili del fuoco	*veejeelee del fwoko*
flood	l'inondazione	*eenondatz-yone*
injured	ferito	*faireeto*
lose	perdere	*pairdaire*

passport	il passaporto	*pas-saporto*
pickpocket	il borsaiolo	*borsi-olo*
police	la polizia	*poleetzee-a*
police station	il commissariato di polizia	*kom-mees-sar-yato dee poleetzee-a*
rob	derubare	*dairoobare*
steal	rubare	*roobare*
theft	il furto	*foorto*
thief	il ladro	*ladro*
tow	rimorchiare	*reemork-yare*

Help!
Aiuto!
I-ooto

Look out!
(Stia) attento!
(stee-a) at-tento

Stop!
Si fermi!
see fairmee

Where is the British embassy?
Dov'è l'ambasciata britannica?
doveh l'amba-shata bree-tan-neeka

This is an emergency!
Questa è un'emergenza!
kwesta eh oon emairjentza

Get an ambulance!
Chiami un'ambulanza!
k-yamee oon amboolantza

Hurry up!
Presto!
presto

Please send an ambulance to …
Per favore, mandate un'ambulanza a …
pair favore mandate oon amboolantza a

Please come to …
Venite, per favore, a …
veneete pair favore a

My address is …
Il mio indirizzo è …
eel mee-o eendeereetzo eh

We've had a break-in
Ci sono entrati i ladri in casa
chee sono entratee ee ladree een kaza

There's a fire at …
C'è un incendio a …
cheh oon eenchend-yo a

Someone's been injured
C'è un ferito
cheh oon faireeto

Someone's been knocked down
È stata investita una persona
eh stata eenvesteeta oona pairsona

He's passed out
È svenuto
eh svenooto

My passport/car has been stolen
Mi hanno rubato il passaporto/la macchina
mee an-no roobato eel pas-saporto/la mak-keena

I've lost my traveller's cheques
Ho perso i miei traveller's cheques
o pairso ee mee-ay 'traveller's cheques'

I want to report a stolen credit card
Vorrei denunciare il furto di una carta di credito
vor-ray denoonchare eel foorto dee oona karta dee kredeeto

It was stolen from my room
È stato rubato dalla mia camera
eh stato roobato dal-la mee-a kamaira

I lost it in the park/at the station
L'ho perso nel parco/alla stazione
lo pairso nel parko/al-la statz-yone

My luggage is missing
I miei bagagli sono spariti
ee mee-ay bagal-yee sono spareetee

Has my luggage been found yet?
Sono stati ritrovati i miei bagagli?
sono statee reetrovatee ee mee-ay bagal-yee

I've crashed my car/had a crash
Ho avuto un incidente con la macchina
oh avooto oon eencheedente kon la mak-keena

My car's been broken into
La mia macchina è stata forzata
la mee-a mak-keena eh stata fortzata

The registration number is …
Il numero di targa è …
eel noomairo dee targa eh

I've been mugged (*said by a man*)
Sono stato aggredito
sono stato ag-gredeeto

(*said by a woman*)
Sono stata aggredita
sono stata ag-gredeeta

My son's missing
Mio figlio è scomparso
mee-o feel-yo eh skomparso

He has fair/brown hair
Ha i capelli biondi/castani
a ee kapel-lee b-yondee/kastanee

He's … years old
Ha … anni
a … an-nee

I've locked myself out *(said by a man)*
Sono rimasto chiuso fuori
sono reemasto k-yoozo fworee

(said by a woman)
Sono rimasta chiusa fuori
sono reemasta k-yooza fworee

He's drowning!
Sta annegando!
sta an-negando

He/she can't swim!
Non sa nuotare!
non sa nwotare

THINGS YOU'LL HEAR

Il suo/vostro indirizzo, prego?
What's your address, please?

Dove si trova/vi trovate?
Where are you?

Può descriverlo?
Can you describe it/him?

THINGS YOU'LL SEE

carabinieri	police
commissariato di polizia	police station
emergenza sanitaria	medical emergency
farmacia di turno	on duty chemist
numeri di emergenza	emergency phone numbers
ospedale	hospital
polizia	police
polizia stradale	traffic police
pronto intervento	emergency service
pronto soccorso	first aid, casualty
soccorso alpino	mountain rescue
soccorso stradale	breakdown service
telefono	telephone
vigili del fuoco	fire brigade

HEALTH

If you are in need of urgent medical attention, go to the **Pronto Soccorso** (casualty) of the nearest hospital.

Various medicines are available in any chemist (**farmacia**), but a prescription may be required. Because of 24-hour service, there is always a chemist open in all cities and most towns. Those that are open at night (**servizio notturno**) are listed in local newspapers and on all chemist's doors.

USEFUL WORDS AND PHRASES

accident	l'incidente	*eencheedente*
ambulance	l'ambulanza	*amboolantza*
anemic	anemico	*anemeeko*
appendicitis	l'appendicite	*ap-pendeecheete*
appendix	l'appendice	*ap-pendeeche*
aspirin	l'aspirina	*aspeereena*
asthma	l'asma	*azma*
backache	il mal di schiena	*mal dee sk-yena*
bandage	la fascia, benda	*fasha, benda*
bite (*by dog, snake*)	il morso	*morso*
(*by insect*)	la puntura	*poontoora*
bladder	la vescica	*vesheeka*
blister	la vescica	*vesheeka*
blood	il sangue	*sangwe*
blood donor	il donatore di sangue	*donatore dee sangwe*
burn	la bruciatura	*broo-chatoora*
cancer	il cancro	*kankro*
chemist	il farmacista	*farmacheesta*
chest	il petto	*pet-to*
chickenpox	la varicella	*vareechel-la*
cold	il raffreddore	*raf-fred-dore*
concussion	la commozione cerebrale	*kom-motz-yone chairebrale*
constipation	la stitichezza	*steeteeketza*

113

contact lenses	le lenti a contatto	_lentee a kontat-to_
corn	il callo	_kal-lo_
cough	la tosse	_tos-se_
cut	il taglio	_tal-yo_
dentist	il dentista	_denteesta_
diabetes	il diabete	_dee-abete_
diarrhoea	la diarrea	_dee-are-a_
doctor	il dottore, il medico	_dot-tore, medeeko_
earache	il mal d'orecchi	_mal dorek-kee_
fever	la febbre	_feb-bre_
filling	l'otturazione	_ot-tooratz-yone_
first aid	il pronto soccorso	_pronto sok-korso_
flu	l'influenza	_eenfloo-entza_
fracture	la frattura	_frat-toora_
German measles	la rosolia	_rozolee-a_
haemorrhage	l'emorragia	_emor-rajee-a_
hangover	la sbornia	_sborneea_
hay fever	il raffreddore da fieno	_raf-fred-dore da f-yeno_
headache	il mal di testa	_mal dee testa_
heart	il cuore	_kwore_
heart attack	l'infarto	_eenfarto_
hepatitis	l'epatite	_epatitee_
HIV positive	HIV positivo	_'HIV' positivo_
hospital	l'ospedale	_ospedale_
indigestion	l'indigestione	_eendeejest-yone_
injection	l'iniezione	_een-yetz-yone_
itch	il prurito	_prooreeto_
kidney	il rene	_rene_
lump	il nodulo	_nodoolo_
measles	il morbillo	_morbeel-lo_
migraine	l'emicrania	_emeekranee-a_
mumps	gli orecchioni	_orekk-yonee_
nausea	la nausea	_now-ze-a_
nurse	l'infermiera	_eenfairmee-aira_
(_male_)	l'infermiere	_eenfairmee-aire_

operation	l'operazione	opairatz-yone
optician	l'ottico	ot-teeko
pain	il dolore	dolore
penicillin	la penicillina	peneecheel-leena
plaster (sticky)	il cerotto	chairot-to
plaster of Paris	il gesso	jes-so
pneumonia	la polmonite	polmoneete
pregnant	incinta	eencheenta
prescription	la ricetta	reechet-ta
rheumatism	il reumatismo	re-oomateezmo
scald	la scottatura	skot-tatoora
scratch	il graffio	graf-fee-o
sick	malato	malato
smallpox	il vaiolo	vi-olo
sore throat	il mal di gola	mal dee gola
splinter	la scheggia	skej-ja
sprain	la slogatura,	zlogatura,
	lo strappo muscolare	strap-po mooskolare
sting	la puntura	poontura
stomach	lo stomaco	stomako
temperature	la febbre	feb-bre
tonsils	le tonsille	tonseel-le
toothache	il mal di denti	mal dee dentee
travel sickness	il mal d'auto	mal dowto
ulcer	l'ulcera	oolchaira
vaccination	la vaccinazione	vacheenatz-yone
vomit (verb)	vomitare	vomeetare
whooping cough	la pertosse	pairtos-se

I have a pain in …
Mi fa male …
mee fa male

I do not feel well
Non mi sento bene
non mee sento bene

I feel faint
Mi sento svenire
mee sento zveneere

I feel sick
Ho la nausea
o la now-ze-a

I feel dizzy
Mi gira la testa
mee jeera la testa

It hurts here
Mi fa male qui
mee fa male kwee

It's a sharp/dull pain
È un dolore acuto/sordo
eh oon dolore akooto/sordo

It hurts all the time
Mi fa continuamente male
mee fa konteenoo-amente male

It only hurts now and then
Non mi fa sempre male
non mee fa sempre male

It hurts when you touch it
Mi fa male quando lo tocca
mee fa male kwando lo tok-ka

It hurts more at night
Mi fa male di più di notte
mee fa male dee p-yoo dee not-te

It stings
Brucia
broocha

It aches
Fa male
fa male

I have a temperature
Ho la febbre
o la feb-bre

I'm … months pregnant
Sono incinta di … mesi
sono eencheenta dee … maisee

Can you take these if you're pregnant/breastfeeding?
Va bene prendere queste quando si è incinta/si sta allattando?
va bene prendaire kwe-ste kwando see e eencheenta/see sta al-lat-tando

I need a prescription for …
Avrei bisogno di una ricetta per …
avray beezon-yo dee oona reechet-ta pair

I normally take …
Generalmente prendo …
jenairalmente prendo

I'm allergic to … *(said by a man/woman)*
Sono allergico/allergica a …
sono al-lairjeeko/al-lairjeeka a

Have you got anything for …?
Ha qualcosa per …?
a kwalkoza pair

Do I need a prescription for …?
C'è bisogno della ricetta per …?
cheh beezon-yo del-la reechet-ta pair

I have lost a filling
Ho perso un'otturazione
oh pairso oon ot-tooratz-yone

Will he/she be all right?
Starà bene?
stara bene

Will he/she need an operation?
Dovrà essere operato/operata?
dovra essaire operato/operata

How is he/she?
Come sta?
kome sta

THINGS YOU'LL SEE

ambulanza	ambulance
anticamera	waiting room
autoambulanza	ambulance
chirurgia	surgery
chirurgo	surgeon
degente	inpatient
dermatologo	dermatologist
dottore	doctor
farmacia di turno	late-night chemist
ginecologo	gynecologist
infermeria	infirmary
medico di turno	doctor on duty
oculista	opthalmologist
orario di visita	visiting hours
ospedale	hospital
otorinolaringoiatra	ear, nose and throat specialist
ottico	optician
pronto soccorso	first aid, casualty
reparto	ward
sala operatoria	operating room
specialista	specialist

THINGS YOU'LL HEAR

Da inghiottire con acqua
To be swallowed with water

Da masticare
Chew them

Una/due/tre volte al giorno
Once/twice/three times a day

Prima di andare a letto
At bedtime

Al mattino
In the morning

Cosa prende normalmente?
What do you normally take?

Penso che lei debba andare dal medico
I think you should see a doctor

Mi dispiace, non ne abbiamo/vendiamo
I'm sorry, we don't have/sell that

Per questo c'è bisogno della ricetta
You need a prescription for that

CONVERSION TABLES

DISTANCES

A mile is 1.6 km. To convert kilometres to miles, divide the km by 8 and multiply by 5. Convert miles to km by dividing the miles by 5 and multiplying by 8.

miles	0.62	1.24	1.86	2.43	3.11	3.73	4.35	6.21
miles *or* **km**	1	2	3	4	5	6	7	10
km	1.61	3.22	4.83	6.44	8.05	9.66	11.27	16.10

WEIGHTS

The kilogram is equivalent to 2 lb 3 oz. To convert kg to lbs, divide by 5 and multiply by 11. One ounce is about 28 grams, and eight ounces about 227 grams; 1 lb is therefore about 454 grams.

lbs	2.20	4.41	6.61	8.82	11.02	13.23	19.84	22.04
lbs *or* **kg**	1	2	3	4	5	6	9	10
kg	0.45	0.91	1.36	1.81	2.27	2.72	4.08	4.53

TEMPERATURE

To convert Celsius degrees into Fahrenheit, the accurate method is to multiply the C° figure by 1.8 and add 32. Similarly, to convert F° to C°, subtract 32 from the F° figure and divide by 1.8.

C°	-10	0	5	10	20	30	36.9	40	100
F°	14	32	41	50	68	86	98.4	104	212

LIQUIDS

A litre is about 1.75 pints; a gallon is roughly 4.5 litres.

gals	0.22	0.44	1.10	2.20	4.40	6.60	11.00
gals *or* **litres**	1	2	5	10	20	30	50
liters	4.54	9.10	22.73	45.46	90.92	136.40	227.30

TYRE PRESSURES

lb/sq in	18	20	22	24	26	28	30	33
kg/sq cm	1.3	1.4	1.5	1.7	1.8	2.0	2.1	2.3

MINI-DICTIONARY

a un/uno/una/un' *(see page 5)*
about: about 16 circa 16
  a book about Venice un libro
  su Venezia
accelerator l'acceleratore
accident l'incidente
accommodation l'alloggio, il posto
ache il dolore
adaptor il riduttore
address l'indirizzo
adhesive l'adesivo
admission charge prezzo d'ingresso
after dopo
afternoon il pomeriggio
aftershave il dopobarba
again di nuovo
against contro
AIDS l'Aids
air l'aria
air conditioning l'aria condizionata
aircraft l'aereo
airline la linea aerea
airport l'aeroporto
airport bus l'autobus navetta
alarm clock la sveglia
alcohol l'alcol
all tutto
  all the streets
  tutte le strade
  that's all questo è tutto
almost quasi
alone solo
Alps le Alpi
already già
always sempre
am: I am (io) sono
ambulance l'ambulanza
America l'America

American *(man)* l'americano
  (woman) l'americana
  (adj.) americano
and e
ankle la caviglia
another un altro, un'altra
answering machine la segreteria
  telefonica
antifreeze l'antigelo
antique shop il negozio
  di antiquariato
antiseptic l'antisettico
apartment l'appartamento
aperitif l'aperitivo
appetite l'appetito
apple la mela
application form il modulo
  per la domanda
appointment l'appuntamento
apricot l'albicocca
are: you are (Lei) è
  (singular, familiar) (tu) sei
  (plural) (voi) siete
  we are (noi) siamo
  they are (loro) sono
arm il braccio
arrive arrivare
art l'arte
art gallery la galleria d'arte
artist l'artista
as: as soon as possible (il) più presto
  possibile
ashtray il portacenere
asleep: he's asleep dorme
aspirin l'aspirina
at: at the post office all'ufficio postale
  at night di notte
  at 3 o'clock alle tre

attractive attraente
aunt la zia
Australia l'Australia
Australian (man) l'australiano
  (woman) l'australiana
  (adj.) australiano
automatic automatico
away: is it far away? è lontano?
  go away! vattene!
awful terribile, orribile
axle il semiasse

baby il bambino
  (female) la bambina
baby wipes i fazzolettini igienici
back (not front) la parte posteriore
  (body) la schiena
  to come back tornare
backpack lo zaino
bacon la pancetta
  bacon and eggs uova e pancetta
bad cattivo
bag la borsa
baggage claim il ritiro bagagli
bait l'esca
bake cuocere (al forno)
bakery la panetteria
balcony il balcone
ball (football etc) la palla,
  il pallone
  (tennis etc) la pallina
ballpoint pen Biro®
banana la banana
band (musicians) la banda
bandage la fascia
  plaster (sticky) il cerotto
bank la banca
banknote la banconota
bar (drinks) il bar
  bar of chocolate
  la tavoletta di cioccolata
barbecue il barbecue
  (occasion) la grigliata all'aperto

barber's il barbiere
bargain l'affare
basement il seminterrato
basket il cestino
  (in supermarket) il cestello
bath il bagno
  (tub) la vasca da bagno
  to have a bath
  fare il bagno
bathing suit il costume da bagno
bathroom il bagno
battery la batteria
beach la spiaggia
beans i fagioli
beard la barba
beautiful bello
because perché
bed il letto
bed linen le lenzuola
bedroom la camera da letto
beef il manzo
beer la birra
before ... prima di ...
beginner il/la principiante
beginners' slope la discesa per
  principianti
behind dietro
  behind ... dietro a ...
beige beige
bell (church) la campana
  (door) il campanello
below sotto
belt la cintura
  (technical) la cinghia
beside ... vicino a ...
best il migliore
better (than) migliore (di)
between ... fra ...
bicycle la bicicletta
big grande
bikini il bikini
bill il conto
bird l'uccello

birthday il compleanno
  happy birthday! buon compleanno!
biscuit il biscotto
bite *(noun: by dog)* il morso
  (by insect) la puntura
  (verb: by dog) mordere
  (by insect) pungere
bitter amaro
black nero
blackberry la mora
blackcurrant il ribes nero
blanket la coperta
bleach la varecchina
  (verb: hair) ossigenare
blind *(cannot see)* cieco
  (on window) la tenda avvolgibile
blizzard la bufera di neve
blond *(adj.)* biondo/bionda
blood il sangue
blouse la camicetta
blue azzurro
  (navy blue) blu
boat la nave
  (small) la barca
  (passenger) il battello
body il corpo
boil *(verb: of water)* bollire
  (egg etc) far bollire
bolt *(noun: on door)* il catenaccio
  (verb) chiudere con il catenaccio
bone l'osso
  (fish) la lisca
book *(noun)* il libro
  (verb) prenotare
booking office la biglietteria
bookshop la libreria
boot lo stivale
border il confine
boring noioso
born: I was born in London
  sono nato a Londra
born: I was born in 1965 sono nato nel
1965

both: both of them tutti e due
  both ... and ... sia ... che ...
bottle la bottiglia
bottle opener l'apribottiglie
bottom il fondo
  (part of body) il sedere
  at the bottom (of) in fondo (a)
bowl la scodella, la ciotola
  (mixing bowl) la terrina
box la scatola
  (of wood etc) la cassetta
box office il botteghino
boy il ragazzo
boyfriend il ragazzo
bra il reggiseno
bracelet il braccialetto
brake *(noun)* il freno
  (verb) frenare
brandy il brandy
bread il pane
breakdown *(car)* il guasto
  (nervous) l'esaurimento nervoso
  I've had a breakdown *(car)* ho avuto
un guasto
breakfast la colazione
breathe respirare
bridge il ponte
  the Bridge of Sighs il Ponte dei Sospiri
briefcase la cartella
British britannico
brochure l'opuscolo
broken rotto
  broken leg la gamba rotta
brooch la spilla
brother il fratello
brown marrone
bruise il livido
brush *(noun: hair)* la spazzola
  (paint) il pennello
  (cleaning) la scopa
  (verb: hair) spazzolare
bucket il secchio
building l'edificio

bumper il paraurti
burglar il ladro
burn (noun) la bruciatura
  (verb) bruciare
bus l'autobus
  (coach) la corriera
business l'affare
  it's none of your business non sono
  affari tuoi
bus station la stazione degli autobus
  la stazione delle corriere
busy (occupied) occupato
  (bar) animato
but ma
butcher's shop la macelleria
butter il burro
button il bottone
buy comprare
by: by the window vicino alla finestra
  by Friday entro venerdì
  by myself da solo
  written by ... scritto da ...

cabbage il cavolo
cable car la funivia
cable/satellite TV TV cavo/satellite
café il caffè, il bar
cake la torta
calculator il calcolatore
call: what's it called? come si chiama?
camcorder la videocamera
camera la macchina fotografica
campsite il campeggio
camshaft l'albero a camme
can (vessel) la lattina
can: can I have ...? posso avere ...?
  can you ...? potreste ...?
  he/she can't ... non può ...
can opener l'apriscatole
Canada il Canada
Canadian (man) il canadese
  (woman) la canadese
  (adj.) canadese

canal il canale
candle la candela
canoe la canoa
cap (bottle) il tappo
  (hat) il berretto
car l'auto, la macchina
carburettor il carburatore
card (for birthday etc) il biglietto di auguri
  playing cards le carte da gioco
cardigan il cardigan
careful attento
  be careful! stia attento!
caretaker il portinaio
  (female) la portinaia
carpet il tappeto
carrot la carota
carry out: to carry out da portare via
car seat (for a baby) il seggiolino per
  macchina
case (suitcase) la valigia
cash (noun) il denaro, gli spicci
  (verb) riscuotere
  to pay cash pagare in contanti
cash machine lo sportello automatico
cassette la cassetta
cassette player il mangianastri
castle il castello
cat il gatto
cathedral la cattedrale
Catholic cattolico
cauliflower il cavolfiore
cave la grotta
cemetery il cimitero
centre il centro
central heating il riscaldamento centrale
certificate il certificato
chair la sedia
change (noun: money) il cambio, gli spicci
  (verb: money, trains) cambiare
  (clothes) cambiarsi
cheap economico, a buon mercato
check-in il check-in
check in (verb) fare il check-in

cheers! (toast) alla salute!, cin cin!
cheese il formaggio
chemist la farmacia
cheque l'assegno
chequebook il libretto degli assegni
cherry la ciliegia
chess gli scacchi
chest (part of body) il petto
  (furniture) il baule
chest of drawers il cassettone
chewing gum il chewing-gum
chicken il pollo
child il bambino
  (female) la bambina
children i bambini
china la porcellana
chips la patatine fritte
chocolate la cioccolata
  box of chocolates una scatola di
  cioccolatini
chop (food) la costoletta
  (verb: cut) tagliare (a pezzetti)
church la chiesa
cigar il sigaro
cigarette la sigaretta
cinema il cinema
city la città
city centre il centro (della città)
class la classe
classical music la musica classica
clean (adj.) pulito
clear (obvious) chiaro
  (water) limpido
clever bravo, intelligente
clingfilm la pellicola adesiva
clock l'orologio
close (near) vicino (a)
  (stuffy) soffocante
  (verb) chiudere
closed chiuso
clothes i vestiti
clubs (cards) fiori
clutch la frizione

coat il capotto
coat hanger l'attaccapanni
cockroach lo scarafaggio
coffee il caffè
coin la moneta
cold (illness) il raffreddore
  (adj.) freddo
  I have a cold ho un raffreddore
Coliseum il Colosseo
collar il colletto
  (for dog) il collare
colleague il collega
collection (stamps etc) la collezione
  (postal) la levata
colour il colore
colour film il rullino a colori
comb (noun) il pettine
  (verb) pettinare
come venire
  I come from ... sono di ...
  we came last week siamo arrivati la
  settimana scorsa
  come here! vieni qui!
compact disk il compact disc
compartment lo scompartimento
complicated complicato
computer il computer
concert il concerto
conditioner (hair) il balsamo
condom il preservativo
conductor (bus) il bigliettaio
  (orchestra) il direttore
congratulations! congratulazioni!
consulate il consolato
contact lenses le lenti a contatto
contraceptive il contraccettivo
cook (noun) il cuoco
  (female) la cuoca
  (verb) cucinare
cooker il fornello
cooking utensils gli utensili da cucina
cool fresco
cork il tappo

corkscrew il cavatappi
corner l'angolo
corridor il corridoio
cosmetics i cosmetici
cost *(verb)* costare
  what does it cost? quanto costa?
cotton il cotone
cotton wool il cotone idrofilo
cough *(noun)* la tosse
  (verb) tossire
country *(state)* il paese
  (not town) la campagna
cousin il cugino
  (female) la cugina
crab il granchio
cramp il crampo
crayfish il gambero
crazy pazzo
cream *(for cake etc)* la crema,
  la panna
  (lotion) la crema
credit card la carta di credito
crew l'equipaggio
crisps le patatine
crowded affollato
cruise la crociera
crutches le stampelle
cry *(verb: weep)* piangere
  (shout) gridare
cucumber il cetriolo
cuff links i gemelli
cup la tazza
cupboard l'armadio
curlers i bigodini
curls i ricci
curry il curry
curtain la tenda
customs la dogana
cut *(noun)* il taglio
  (verb) tagliare

dad il papà, il babbo
damp umido

dance *(noun)* il ballo
  (verb) ballare
dangerous pericoloso
dark scuro
daughter la figlia
day il giorno
dead morto
deaf sordo
dear caro
debit card la carta assegni
deep profondo
delayed in ritardo
deliberately deliberatamente
dentist il/la dentista
dentures la dentiera
deodorant il deodorante
department store il grande magazzino
departure la partenza
departure lounge la sala d'attesa
develop *(film)* sviluppare
diamond *(jewel)* il diamante
diary il diario
dictionary il dizionario
die morire
diesel il diesel
different diverso
  that's different! è diverso!
  I'd like a different one
  ne vorrei un altro
difficult difficile
dining room la sala da pranzo
dinner la cena
directory *(telephone)*
  la guida telefonica
dirty sporco
disabled invalido
dishtowel lo strofinaccio
dishwasher la rondella
distributor *(in car)* il distributore
dive *(noun)* il tuffo
  (verb) tuffarsi
diving board il trampolino
divorced divorziato

do fare
  how do you do?
    piacere di conoscerla
dock il molo
doctor il dottore
  (female) la dottoressa
document il documento
dog il cane
doll la bambola
dollar il dollaro
door la porta
double room la camera doppia
doughnut il krapfen
down giù
drawing pin la puntina da disegno
dress il vestito
drink *(noun)* la bibita
  (verb) bere
  would you like a drink? vorresti
  qualcosa da bere?
drinking water l'acqua potabile
drive *(verb)* guidare
driver il guidatore
  (female) la guidatrice
  (of bus, truck etc) l'autista
driving licence la patente di guida
drunk ubriaco
dry asciutto
  (wine) secco
dry cleaner's la lavanderia a secco
dummy *(for baby)* il ciuccio
during durante
dustbin la pattumiera
duster lo straccio per la polvere
duty-free il duty free
duvet il piumino

each *(every)* ogni
  twenty euros each venti euro ciascuno
ear l'orecchio
  ears le orecchie
early presto
earrings gli orecchini

east l'est
easy facile
eat mangiare
egg l'uovo
either: either of them l'uno o l'altro
  either ... or ... o ... o ...
elastic elastico
elbow il gomito
electric elettrico
electricity l'elettricità
else: something else qualcos'altro
  someone else qualcun'altro
  somewhere else da qualche altra parte
email la posta elettronica
email address l'indirizzo di posta
  elettronica
embarrassing imbarazzante
embassy l'ambasciata
embroidery il ricamo
emergency l'emergenza
emergency brake il freno d'emergenza
emergency exit l'uscita di sicurezza
empty vuoto
end la fine
engaged *(couple)* fidanzato/fidanzata
engine *(car)* il motore
  (train) la locomotiva
England l'Inghilterra
English inglese
Englishman l'inglese
Englishwoman l'inglese
enlargement l'ampliamento
enough abbastanza
entrance l'entrata
envelope la busta
eraser la gomma
escalator la scala mobile
especially particolarmente
estate agent l'agente immobiliare
evening la sera
every ogni
everyone ognuno, tutti
everything tutto

everywhere dappertutto
example l'esempio
  for example per esempio
excellent ottimo, eccellente
excess baggage il bagaglio in eccesso
exchange *(verb)* scambiare
exchange rate il tasso di cambio
excursion l'escursione
excuse me! *(to get past)* permesso!
  (to get attention) mi scusi!
  (when sneezing etc) scusate!
exit l'uscita
expensive caro, costoso
extension lead la prolunga
eye l'occhio
  eyes gli occhi

face la faccia
faint *(unclear)* indistinto
  (verb) svenire
fair *(funfair)* il luna park
  (trade) la fiera
  it's not fair non è giusto
false teeth la dentiera
family la famiglia
fan *(ventilator)* il ventilatore
  (enthusiast) l'ammiratore
fan belt la cinghia della ventola
fantastic fantastico
far lontano
  how far is it to …? quanto dista
  da qui …?
fare la tariffa
farm la fattoria
farmer l'agricoltore
fashion la moda
fast veloce
fat *(person)* grasso
  (on meat etc) il grasso
father il padre
fax *(noun)* il fax
  (verb: document) spedire via fax
fax machine il fax

feel *(touch)* tastare
  I feel hot ho caldo
  I feel like … ho voglia di …
  I don't feel well non mi sento bene
felt-tip pen il pennarello
fence lo steccato
ferry il traghetto
fever la febbre
fiancé il fidanzato
fiancée la fidanzata
field il campo
filling *(in tooth)* l'otturazione
  (in sandwich, cake etc) il ripieno
film *(for camera)* la pellicola
  (at the cinema) il film
filter il filtro
finger il dito
fire il fuoco
  (blaze) l'incendio
fire extinguisher l'estintore
fireworks i fuochi d'artificio
first primo
first aid il pronto soccorso
first floor il primo piano
first name il nome di battesimo
fish il pesce
fishing la pesca
  to go fishing andare a pesca
fishmonger's il pescivendolo
fizzy frizzante
flag la bandiera
flash *(camera)* il flash
flat *(level)* piatto
flavour il gusto
flea la pulce
flight il volo
flip-flops gli infradito
flippers le pinne
floor *(storey)* il piano
  (ground) il pavimento
flour la farina
Florence Firenze
flower il fiore

flute il flauto
fly (insect) la mosca
  (verb) volare
  I'm flying to London
  vado a Londra in aereo
fog la nebbia
folk music la musica folk
food il cibo
food poisoning l'intossicazione
  alimentare
foot il piede
football (game) il calcio
  (ball) il pallone
for per
  for me per me
  what for? perché?
foreigner lo straniero,
  il forestiero
forest la foresta
forget dimenticare
fork (for food) la forchetta
fourth quarto
France la Francia
free (not occupied) libero
  (no charge) gratis
freezer il congelatore
French francese
Frenchman il francese
Frenchwoman la francese
fridge il frigorifero
friend l'amico
  (female) l'amica
friendly cordiale
fringe (hair) la frangia
front: in front of you davanti a te
frost il gelo
fruit la frutta
fruit juice il succo di frutta
fry friggere
frying pan la padella
full pieno
  I'm full (up) sono sazio
full board la pensione completa

funny divertente
  (odd) strano
furniture i mobili

garage il garage
garden il giardino
garlic l'aglio
gas la benzina
gas-permeable lenses le lenti semi-rigide
gas station la stazione di servizio
gate il cancello
  (at airport) l'uscita
gay (homosexual) omosessuale, gay
gear (car) il cambio
gear lever la leva del cambio
gel (hair) il gel
Genoa Genova
German (man) il tedesco
  (woman) la tedesca
  (adj.) tedesco
Germany la Germania
get (obtain) ricevere
  (fetch: person) chiamare
  (something) prendere
  have you got ...? ha ...?
  to get the train prendere il treno
get back: we get back tomorrow
  torniamo domani
  to get something back riavere indietro
  qualcosa
get in entrare
  (arrive) arrivare
get off (bus etc) scendere (da)
get on (bus etc) salire (su)
get out uscire (da)
get up alzarsi
gift il regalo
gin il gin
ginger (spice) lo zenzero
girl la ragazza
girlfriend la ragazza
give dare
glad contento

glass (*material*) il vetro
  (*for drinking*) il bicchiere
glasses gli occhiali
glossy prints le fotografie su carta
  lucida
gloves i guanti
glue la colla
go andare
  (*depart*) partire
gold l'oro
good buono
  good! bene!
goodbye arrivederci
government il governo
granddaughter la nipote
grandfather il nonno
grandmother la nonna
grandparents i nonni
grandson il nipote
grapes l'uva
grass l'erba
Great Britain la Gran Bretagna
Greece la Grecia
Greek (*man*) il greco
  (*woman*) la greca
  (*adj.*) greco
green verde
grey grigio
grill la griglia
grocer's l'alimentari
ground sheet il telone impermeabile
ground floor il pianterreno
guarantee (*noun*) la garanzia
  (*verb*) garantire
guard la guardia
guide (*person*) la guida
guidebook la guida
guitar la chitarra
gun (*rifle*) il fucile
  (*pistol*) la pistola

hair i capelli
haircut il taglio

hairdresser's il parrucchiere
hair dryer il fohn
hairspray la lacca per i capelli
half metà
  half an hour mezz'ora
  half board mezza pensione
ham il prosciutto
hamburger l'hamburger
hammer il martello
hand la mano
hand brake il freno a mano
handle (*door*) la maniglia
handsome bello, attraente
hangover i postumi della sbornia
happy felice
harbour il porto
hard duro
  (*difficult*) difficile
hardware store la ferramenta
hat il cappello
have avere
  I don't have ... non ho ...
  have you got ...? ha ...?
  I have to go now
  devo andare adesso
he lui
head la testa
headache il mal di testa
headlights i fari
hear udire, sentire
hearing aid l'apparecchio acustico
heart il cuore
hearts (*cards*) cuori
heater il termosifone
heating il riscaldamento
heavy pesante
heel (*of foot*) il tallone
  (*of shoe*) il tacco
hello ciao
  (*on phone*) pronto
help (*noun*) l'aiuto
  (*verb*) aiutare
hepatitis l'epatite

her: it's for her è per lei
   give it to her daglielo
   her book il suo libro
   her house la sua casa
   her shoes le sue scarpe
   her dresses i suoi vestiti
   it's hers è suo
hi! salve!
high alto
highway code il codice della strada
hill la collina
him: it's for him è per lui
   give it to him daglielo
his: his book il suo libro
   his house la sua casa
   his shoes le sue scarpe
   his socks i suoi calzini
   it's his è suo
history la storia
hitchhike fare l'autostop
HIV positive HIV positivo
hobby il passatempo
home: at home a casa
homeopathy omeopatia
honest onesto
honey il miele
honeymoon la luna di miele
hood *(car)* il cofano
horn *(car)* il clacson
   (animal) il corno
horrible orribile
hospital l'ospedale
hour l'ora
house la casa
how? come?
hungry: I'm hungry ho fame
hurry: I'm in a hurry ho fretta
husband il marito

I io
ice il ghiaccio
ice cream il gelato
ice skates i pattini da ghiaccio

if se
ignition l'accensione
ill malato
immediately immediatamente
impossible impossibile
in: in English in inglese
   in the hotel nell'albergo
   in Venice a Venezia
indicator l'indicatore di direzione
indigestion l'indigestione
infection l'infezione
information le informazioni
inhaler *(for asthma etc)* l'inalatore
injection l'iniezione
injury la ferita
ink l'inchiostro
inner tube la camera d'aria
insect l'insetto
insect repellent l'insettifugo
insomnia l'insonnia
instant coffee il caffè solubile
insurance l'assicurazione
interesting interessante
internet l'internet
interpret interpretare
interpreter l'interprete
invitation l'invito
Ireland l'Irlanda
Irish irlandese
Irishman l'irlandese
Irishwoman l'irlandese
iron *(material)* il ferro
   (for clothes) il ferro da stiro
   (verb) stirare
is: he/she/it is … (lui/lei/esso) è …
island l'isola
it esso
Italian *(man)* l'italiano
   (woman) l'italiana
   (adj.) italiano
   the Italians gli italiani
Italy Italia
its suo

jacket la giacca
jam la marmellata
jazz il jazz
jeans i jeans
jellyfish la medusa
jeweller il gioielliere
job il lavoro
jog *(verb)* fare jogging
  to jog andare a fare jogging
jogging il jogging
joke lo scherzo
journey il viaggio
just *(only)* solo
  it's just arrived
  è appena arrivato

kettle il bollitore
key la chiave
kidney il rene
kilo il chilo
kilometre il chilometro
kitchen la cucina
knee il ginocchio
knife il coltello
knit lavorare a maglia
knitwear la maglieria
know sapere
  (person) conoscere
  I don't know
  non so

label l'etichetta
lace il pizzo
laces *(of shoe)* i lacci
lady la signora
lake il lago
lamb l'agnello
lamp la lampada
lampshade il paralume
land *(noun)* la terra
  (verb) atterrare
language la lingua
large grande

last *(final)* ultimo
  last week la settimana scorsa
  at last! finalmente!
  last name il cognome
late: it's getting late
  si sta facendo tardi
  the bus is late
  l'autobus è in ritardo
later più tardi
laugh ridere
laundry *(place)* la lavanderia
  (dirty clothes) la biancheria
laxative il lassativo
lazy pigro
leaf la foglia
leaflet il volantino
learn imparare
leather la pelle, il cuoio
left *(not right)* sinistra
  there's nothing left non c'è rimasto
  più nulla
left luggage locker
  il desposito bagagli
leg la gamba
lemon il limone
lemonade la limonata
length la lunghezza
lens la lente
less meno
lesson la lezione
letter la lettera
lettuce la lattuga
library la biblioteca
licence la patente
life la vita
lift l'ascensore
light *(noun)* la luce
  (adj.: not heavy) leggero
  (not dark) chiaro
light bulb la lampadina
lighter l'accendino
lighter fuel il gas per accendini
light meter l'esposimetro

like: I like you mi piaci
  I like swimming mi piace nuotare
  it's like ... assomiglia a ...
  like this one come questo
lime *(fruit)* il limoncello
lip balm il burro di cacao
lipstick il rossetto
liqueur il liquore
list l'elenco
litre il litro
litter i rifiuti
little *(small)* piccolo
  it's a little big è un po' grande
  just a little solo un po'
liver il fegato
lollipop il lecca lecca
long lungo
  how long does it take? quanto ci vuole?
long-distance *(call)* interurbana
lost property l'ufficio oggetti smarriti
lot: a lot molto
loud forte
  (colour) vivo
lounge chair la sedia a sdraio
love *(verb)* amare
lover l'amante
low basso
luck la fortuna
  good luck! buona fortuna!
luggage i bagagli
luggage rack la reticella (per i bagagli)
lunch il pranzo

magazine la rivista
make fare
makeup il trucco
man l'uomo
manager il direttore
  (female) la direttrice
many: not many non molti
map la carta (geografica)
  a map of Rome
  una piantina di Roma

marble il marmo
margarine la margarina
market il mercato
marmalade la marmellata d'arance
married sposato
mascara il mascara
mass *(church)* la messa
mast l'albero
match *(light)* il fiammifero
  (sport) l'incontro
material *(cloth)* la stoffa
matter: it doesn't matter
  non importa
mattress il materasso
maybe forse
me: it's me sono io
  it's for me è per me
  give it to me dammelo
meal il pasto
mean: what does this mean?
  che cosa significa?
meat la carne
mechanic il meccanico
medicine la medicina
Mediterranean il Mediterraneo
meeting l'incontro
melon il melone
menu il menù
message il messaggio
middle: in the middle of the square
  in mezzo alla piazza
  in the middle of the night nel cuore
  della notte
midnight mezzanotte
Milan Milano
milk il latte
mine: it's mine è mio
mineral water l'acqua minerale
minute il minuto
mirror lo specchio
Miss Signorina
mistake l'errore
mobile phone il telefonino

modem il modem
money i soldi
month il mese
monument il monumento
moon la luna
moped il motorino
more: more than ... più di ...
  I want some more
  ne voglio ancora
morning la mattina
  in the morning di mattina
mosaic il mosaico
mosquito la zanzara
mother la madre
motorboat il motoscafo
motorcycle la motocicletta
motorway l'autostrada
mountain la montagna
mountain bike il mountain bike
mouse il topo
mousse *(for hair)* la schiuma
moustache i baffi
mouth la bocca
move *(verb)* muovere
  (move house) traslocare
  don't move! non muoverti!
Mr Signor
Mrs Signora
much: much better molto meglio
  much slower
  molto più lentamente
  not much non molto
mug il tazzone
mum mamma
museum il museo
mushroom il fungo
music la musica
musical instrument lo strumento
  musicale
musician il musicista
mussels le cozze
must: I must devo
mustard la senape

my: my book il mio libro
  my bag la mia borsa
  my keys le mie chiavi
  my dresses i miei vestiti

nail *(metal)* il chiodo
  (finger) l'unghia
nail clippers il tagliaunghie
nailfile la limetta per le unghie
nail polish lo smalto per le unghie
name il nome
  what's your name?
  come ti chiami?
napkin gli assorbenti (igienici)
Naples Napoli
nappies i pannolini
  (disposable) i pannolini usa e getta
narrow stretto
near: near the door
  vicino alla porta
necessary necessario
neck il collo
necklace la collana
need: I need ... ho bisogno di ...
  there's no need non c'è bisogno
needle l'ago
negative *(photo)* la negativa
  (adj.) negativo
neither: neither of them nè l'uno nè
  l'altro
  neither ... nor ... nè ... nè ...
nephew il nipote
never mai
  I never smoke non fumo mai
new nuovo
news le notizie
  (on radio) il notiziario
news agent's il giornalaio
newspaper il giornale
New Zealand la Nuova Zelanda
New Zealander *(man)* il neozelandese
  (woman) la neozelandese
  (adj.) neozelandese

next prossimo
  next week la settimana prossima
  what next? e poi?
  who's next? a chi tocca?
nice *(attractive)* carino, bello
  (pleasant) simpatico
  (to eat) buono
niece la nipote
night la notte
nightclub il night
nightdress la camicia da notte
night porter il portiere di notte
no *(response)* no
  I have no money non ho soldi
nobody nessuno
noisy rumoroso
noon mezzogiorno
north il nord
Northern Ireland l'Irlanda del Nord
nose il naso
not non
  he's not ... non è ...
notebook il quaderno
nothing niente
novel il romanzo
now ora, adesso
nowhere da nessuna parte
nudist il/la nudista
number il numero
number plate la targa
nut la noce, la nocciola
  (for bolt) il dado

oars i remi
occasionally ogni tanto
occupied occupato
octopus la piovra, il polipo
of di
office l'ufficio
often spesso
oil l'olio
ointment l'unguento
OK OK

old vecchio
  how old are you? quanti anni hai?
olive l'oliva
olive oil l'olio d'oliva
omelette l'omelette
on su
  on the table sul tavolo
  a book on Venice un libro su Venezia
  on Monday di lunedì
one uno
onion la cipolla
only solo
open *(adj.)* aperto
  (verb) aprire
operation l'operazione
operator l'operatore
  (female) l'operatrice
opposite: opposite the hotel di fronte
all'albergo
optician l'ottico
or o
orange *(fruit)* l'arancia
  (colour) arancione
orange juice il succo d'arancia
orchestra l'orchestra
ordinary normale
organ *(music)* l'organo
other: the other (one) l'altro
our: our hotel il nostro albergo
  our car la nostra macchina
  it's ours è nostro
out: he's out è uscito
outside fuori
oven il forno
over *(above)* su, sopra
  over 100 più di cento
  over the river al di là del fiume
  it's over *(finished)* è finito
  over there laggiù

pack of cards il mazzo di carte
package il pacchetto
packet il pacchetto

padlock il lucchetto
Padua Padova
page la pagina
pain il dolore
paint la vernice
pair il paio
palace il palazzo
pale pallido
paper la carta
  (newspaper) il giornale
paraffin la paraffina
pardon? prego?
parents i genitori
park *(noun)* il parco
  (verb) parcheggiare
parking lights le luci di posizione
parsley il prezzemolo
part *(hair)* la riga
party *(celebration)* la festa
  (group) il gruppo
  (political) il partito
pass *(driving)* sorpassare
passenger il passeggero
  (female) la passeggera
passport il passaporto
pasta la pasta
pastry store la pasticceria
path il sentiero
pavement il marciapiede
pay pagare
peach la pesca
peanuts le arachidi,
pear la pera
pearl la perla
peas i piselli
pedestrian il pedone
peg *(clothes)* la molletta
pen la penna
pencil la matita
pencil sharpener il temperamatite
pen friend il/la corrispondente
penknife il temperino
people la gente

pepper il pepe
  (red, green) il peperone
peppermint la menta piperita
per: per person a persona
  per annum all'anno
perfect perfetto
perfume il profumo
perhaps forse
perm la permanente
phonecard la scheda telefonica
photocopier la fotocopiatrice
photograph *(noun)* la fotografia
  (verb) fotografare
photographer il fotografo
phrase book il vocabolarietto
pickpocket il borsaiolo
picnic il picnic
piece il pezzo
pillow il cuscino
pin lo spillo
pineapple l'ananas
pink rosa
pipe *(for smoking)* la pipa
  (for water) il tubo
piston il pistone
pizza la pizza
place il posto
  at your place a casa tua
plant la pianta
plastic la plastica
plastic bag il sacchetto di plastica
plate il piatto
platform il binario
play *(theatre)* la commedia
  (verb) giocare
please per favore
plug *(electrical)* la spina
  (sink) il tappo
pocket la tasca
poison il veleno
police la polizia
police officer il poliziotto
police station la stazione di polizia

politics la politica
poor povero
  poor quality di cattiva qualità
Pope il Papa
pop music la musica pop
pork la carne di maiale
port il porto
porter *(hotel)* il portiere
possible possibile
post *(noun)* la posta
  (verb) spedire per posta
post box la bucca delle lettere
postcard la cartolina
poster il manifesto
postman il postino
post office l'ufficio postale
potato la patata
poultry il pollame
pound *(weight)* la libbra
powder *(cosmetic)* la cipria
pram la carrozzina
prefer preferire
prescription la ricetta
pretty *(beautiful)* grazioso, carino
  (quite) piuttosto
priest il prete
private privato
problem il problema
public pubblico
pull tirare
puncture la foratura
purple viola
purse il borsellino
push spingere
pushchair il passegino
put mettere
pyjamas il pigiama

quality la qualità
quarter il quarto
question la domanda
queue *(noun)* la fila
  (verb) fare la fila

quick veloce
quiet tranquillo
quite *(fairly)* abbastanza
  (fully) molto

radiator il radiatore
radio la radio
radish il ravanello
railway la ferrovia
rain la pioggia
raincoat l'impermeabile
raisins l'uvetta
rare *(uncommon)* raro
  (steak) al sangue
raspberry il lampone
rat il ratto
razor blades le lamette
read leggere
reading lamp la lampada da studio
ready pronto
rear lights i fari posteriort
receipt *(restaurants, hotels)* la ricevuta
  (shops, bars) lo scontrino
receptionist il/la receptionist
record *(music)* il disco
  (sports etc) il record
record shop il negozio di dischi
red rosso
refreshments i rinfreschi
relax rilassarsi
religion la religione
remember ricordare
  I don't remember non ricordo
rent *(verb: apartment)* affittare
reservation la prenotazione
rest *(noun: remainder)* il resto
  (verb: relax) riposarsi
restaurant il ristorante
return ritornare
  (give back) restituire
return ticket il biglietto di andata e
  ritorno
rice il riso

rich ricco
right *(correct)* giusto, esatto
  (not left) destro
ring *(noun: wedding etc)* l'anello
ripe maturo
river il fiume
road la strada
rock *(stone)* la roccia
  (music) il rock
roll *(bread)* il panino
Roman Forum il Foro Romano
Rome Roma
roof il tetto
room la stanza
  (space) lo spazio
rope la corda
rose la rosa
round *(circular)* rotondo
  it's my round tocca a me offrire
row remare
rowing boat la barca a remi
rubber band l'elastico
rubbish le immondizie,
  la spazzatura
rubbish bag il sacchetto per la
  pattumiera
ruby *(stone)* il rubino
rug *(mat)* il tappeto
ruins le rovine, i resti
ruler *(for drawing)* la riga
rum il rum
run *(verb)* correre

sad triste
safe *(not dangerous)* sicuro
safety pin la spilla di sicurezza
St Mark's Square Piazza San Marco
St Peter's San Pietro
salad l'insalata
salami il salame
sale *(at reduced prices)* i saldi
salmon il salmone
salt il sale

same: the same dress lo stesso vestito
  same again, please un altro, per favore
sand la sabbia
sandals i sandali
sand dunes le dune
sandwich il panino
sanitary towels gli assorbenti (igienici)
Sardinia la Sardegna
sauce la salsa
saucepan la pentola
sauna la sauna
sausage la salsiccia
say dire
  what did you say? che cosa ha detto?
  how do you say …? come si dice …?
scarf la sciarpa
  (head) il foulard
school la scuola
scissors le forbici
Scotland la Scozia
Scotsman lo scozzese
Scotswoman la scozzese
Scottish scozzese
screw la vite
screwdriver il cacciavite
sea il mare
seafood i frutti di mare
seat il posto
seat belt la cintura di sicurezza
second secondo
see vedere
  I can't see non vedo
  I see capisco, vedo
sell vendere
separate *(adj.)* separato
separated *(couple)* separati
serious serio
several diversi
sew cucire
shampoo lo shampoo
shave: to shave radersi
shaving cream la schiuma da barba
shawl lo scialle

she lei
sheet il lenzuolo
shell la conchiglia
shellfish *(crabs etc)* i crostacei
  (molluscs) i molluschi
sherry lo sherry
ship la nave
shirt la camicia
shoelaces i lacci per le scarpe
shoe polish il lucido per le scarpe
shoes le scarpe
shop il negozio
shopping la spesa
  to go shopping
  andare a fare acquisti
  (for food) andare a fare la spesa
short corto
shorts gli short,
  i pantaloncini corti
shoulder la spalla
shower la doccia
  (rain) l'acquazzone
shower gel la docciaschiuma
shutter *(camera)* l'otturatore
  (window) l'imposta, le persiane
Sicily la Sicilia
side *(edge)* il lato
sights: the sights of …
  le attrazioni turistiche di …
silk la seta
silver *(colour)* d'argento
  (metal) l'argento
simple semplice
sing cantare
single *(one)* solo
  (unmarried: man) celibe
  (woman) nubile
single room la camera singola
single ticket il biglietto di sola andata
sink il lavabo, il lavandino
sister la sorella
skid slittare
skiing: to go skiing andare a sciare

skin cleanser il latte detergente
ski resort la località sciistica
skirt la gonna
skis gli sci
sky il cielo
sleep *(noun)* il sonno
  (verb) dormire
sleeping bag il sacco a pelo
sleeping car il vagone letto
sleeping pill il sonnifero
slippers le pantofole
slow lento
small piccolo
smell *(noun)* l'odore
  (verb: stink) puzzare
smile *(noun)* il sorriso
  (verb) sorridere
smoke *(noun)* il fumo
  (verb) fumare
snack lo spuntino
snorkel il boccaglio
snow la neve
so: so good così bene
  not so much non così tanto
soaking solution *(for contact lenses)*
  il liquido per lenti
soap il sapone
socks i calzini
soda water l'acqua di seltz
somebody qualcuno
somehow in qualche modo
something qualcosa
sometimes qualche volta
somewhere da qualche parte
son il figlio
song la canzone
sorry! scusi!
  I'm sorry mi dispiace
  sorry? *(pardon)* come?, scusi?
soup la zuppa
south il sud
souvenir il souvenir
spade *(shovel)* la vanga

spades *(cards)* picche
Spain la Spagna
Spanish spagnolo
spare parts *(car)* i pezzi di ricambio
spark plug la candela
speak parlare
  do you speak …? parla …?
  I don't speak … non parlo …
speed la velocità
SPF (sun protection factor) il fattore di
  protezione
spider il ragno
spinach gli spinaci
spoon il cucchiaio
spring *(mechanical)* la molla
  (season) la primavera
square *(noun: in town)* la piazza
  (adj.: shape) quadrato
staircase la scala
stairs le scale
stamp il francobollo
stapler la cucitrice
star la stella
  (film) la star
start *(noun)* l'inizio
  (verb) cominciare
station la stazione
statue la statua
steal rubare
  it's been stolen
  è stato rubato
steamer *(boat)* la nave a vapore
  (for cooking) la pentola a pressione
stockings le calze
stomach lo stomaco
stomachache il mal di stomaco
stop *(noun: bus)* la fermata dell'autobus
  (verb) fermare
  stop! alt!, fermo!
storm la tempesta
strawberry la fragola
stream il ruscello
street la strada

string *(cord)* lo spago
  (guitar etc) la corda
strong forte
student lo studente
  (female) la studentessa
stupid stupido
suburbs la periferia
sugar lo zucchero
suit *(noun)* il completo
  it suits you ti sta bene
suitcase la valigia
sun il sole
sunbathe prendere il sole
sunburn la scottatura
sunglasses gli occhiali da sole
sunny: it's sunny c'è il sole
sunshade l'ombrellone
suntan: to get a suntan abbronzarsi
suntan lotion la lozione solare
suntanned abbronzato
supermarket il supermercato
supper la cena
supplement il supplemento
sure sicuro
  are you sure? sei sicuro?
sweat *(noun)* il sudore
  (verb) sudare
sweater il maglione
sweatshirt la felpa
sweet la caramella
  (not sour) dolce
swim *(verb)* nuotare
swimming pool la piscina
swimming trunks
  il costume da bagno *(per uomo)*
Swiss *(man)* lo svizzero
  (woman) la svizzera
  (adj.) svizzero
switch l'interruttore
Switzerland la Svizzera
synagogue la sinagoga

table il tavolo
tablet la compressa
take prendere
takeoff il decollo
talcum powder il talco
talk *(noun)* la conversazione
    (verb) parlare
tall alto
tampons i tamponi
tangerine il mandarino
tap il rubinetto
tapestry l'arazzo
teacher l'insegnante
telephone *(noun)* il telefono
    (verb) telefonare
telephone booth la cabina telefonica
telephone call la telefonata
television la televisione
temperature la temperatura
    (fever) la febbre
tent la tenda
tent pole il palo della tenda
than di
thank *(verb)* ringraziare
    thank you/thanks grazie
that: that one quello
    that country quel paese
    that man quell'uomo
    that woman quella donna
    what's that? cos'è quello?
    I think that … penso che …
the *(see page 5)*
their: their room la loro stanza
    their friend il loro amico
    their books i loro libri
    their pens le loro penne
    it's theirs è loro
them: it's for them è per loro
    give it to them dallo a loro
then poi, allora
there là
    there is/are … c'è/ci sono …
    is/are there …? c'è/ci sono …?

these: these things queste cose
    these boys questi ragazzi
they loro
thick spesso
thin sottile
think pensare
    I think so penso di sì
    I'll think about it ci penserò
third terzo
thirsty: I'm thirsty ho sete
this: this one questo
    this picture questo quadro
    this man quest'uomo
    this woman questa donna
    what's this? cos'è questo?
    this is Mr … (questo è) il signor …
those: those things quelle cose
    those boys quei ragazzi
throat la gola
throat pastilles le pasticche per la gola
through attraverso
thunderstorm il temporale
Tiber il Tevere
ticket il biglietto
ticket office la biglietteria
tide la marea
tie *(noun)* la cravatta
    (verb) legare
tight *(clothes)* stretto
tights *(sheer)* i collant
    (wool) la calzamaglia
time il tempo
    what's the time? che ore sono?
timetable l'orario
tin la scatola
tip *(money)* la mancia
    (end) la punta
tired stanco
tissues i fazzolettini di carta
to: to England in Inghilterra
    to the station alla stazione
    to the doctor dal dottore
    to the centre in centro

toast il pane tostato
tobacco il tabacco
today oggi
together insieme
toilet la toilette
toilet *(men's)* la toilette degli uomini
  (women's) la toilette delle donne
toilet paper la carta igienica
tomato il pomodoro
tomato juice il succo di pomodoro
tomorrow domani
tongue la lingua
tonic l'acqua tonica
tonight stasera
too *(also)* anche
  (excessively) troppo
tooth il dente
toothache il mal di denti
toothbrush lo spazzolino da denti
toothpaste il dentifricio
torch la torcia elettrica
tour il giro
tourist il/la turista
tourist office l'ufficio turistico
towel l'asciugamano
tower la torre
  Leaning Tower of Pisa la Torre di Pisa
town la città
town hall il municipio
toy il giocattolo
toy shop il negozio di giocattoli
track suit la tuta da ginnastica
tractor il trattore
tradition la tradizione
traffic il traffico
traffic jam l'ingorgo
traffic lights il semaforo
trailer il rimorchio, la roulotte
train il treno
trainers le scarpe da ginnastica
translate tradurre
translator il traduttore
  (female) la traduttrice

travel agency l'agenzia di viaggio
traveller's cheque il traveller's cheque
tray il vassoio
tree l'albero
trousers i pantaloni
truck il camion
true vero
try provare
Turin Torino
tunnel il tunnel
Tuscany la Toscana
tweezers le pinzette
typewriter la macchina da scrivere
tyre la gomma

umbrella l'ombrello
uncle lo zio
under ... sotto ...
underground la metropolitana
underpants le mutande
underskirt la sottoveste
understand capire
  I don't understand non capisco
underwear la biancheria intima
university l'università
unleaded senza piombo
until fino a
unusual insolito
up su
  (upward) verso l'alto
  up there lassù
urgent urgente
us: it's for us è per noi
  give it to us daccelo
use *(noun)* l'uso
  (verb) usare
  it's no use non serve a niente
useful utile
usual solito
usually di solito

vacancy *(room)* la stanza libera
vacation la vacanza

valley la valle
valve la valvola
vanilla la vaniglia
vase il vaso
Vatican City la Città del Vaticano
VCR il videoregistratore
veal la carne di vitello
vegetables la verdura
vegetarian vegetariano
vehicle il veicolo
Venice Venezia
very molto
  very much moltissimo
vest la canottiera
video (tape/film) il video cassetta
view la vista
viewfinder il mirino
villa la villa
village il villaggio
violin il violino
visit (noun) la visita
  (verb) andare a trovare
visitor l'ospite
vitamin pill la compressa di vitamine
vodka la vodka
voice la voce

wait aspettare
  wait! aspetta!
waiter il cameriere
  waiter! cameriere!
waiting room la sala d'attesa
waitress la cameriera
  waitress! cameriera!
Wales il Galles
walk (noun: stroll) la passeggiata
  (verb) camminare
  to go for a walk andare a fare una
  passeggiata
wall il muro
wallet il portafoglio
war la guerra
wardrobe il guardaroba, l'armadio

warm caldo
was: I was (io) ero
  he/she/it was (lui/lei/esso) era
washing powder il detersivo (per bucato)
washing-up liquid il detersivo
  liquido per piatti
wasp la vespa
watch (noun) l'orologio
  (verb) guardare
water l'acqua
waterfall la cascata
water heater lo scaldabagno
wave (noun) l'onda
  (verb: with hand) salutare
wavy: wavy hair i capelli ondulati
we noi
weather il tempo
Web site il sito internet
wedding il matrimonio
week la settimana
welcome benvenuto
  you're welcome di niente, prego
Wellington boots gli stivali do gomma
Welsh gallese
Welshman il gallese
Welshwoman la gallese
were: you were (Lei) era
  (singular, familiar) (tu) eri
  (plural) (voi) eravate
  we were (noi) eravamo
  they were (loro) erano
west l'ovest
wet bagnato
what? cosa?
wheel la ruota
wheelchair la sedia a rotelle
when? quando?
where? dove?
whether se
which? quale?
whisky il whisky
white bianco
who? chi?

why? perchè?
wide ampio
wife la moglie
wind il vento
window la finestra
windscreen il parabrezza
wine il vino
wing l'ala
with con
without senza
woman la donna
wood (*material*) il legno
wool la lana
word la parola
work (*noun*) il lavoro
   (*verb*) lavorare
   (*machine*) funzionare
worse peggiore
worst il peggiore
wrench la chiave fissa
wrapping paper la carta da imballaggio
   (*for presents*) la carta da regalo
wrist il polso
writing paper la carta da scrivere
wrong sbagliato

year l'anno
yellow giallo
yes sì
yesterday ieri
yet ancora
   not yet non ancora
yoghurt lo yogurt
you Lei
   (*singular, familiar*) tu
   (*plural*) voi
your: (*singular, formal*)
   your book il suo libro
   your shirt la sua camicia
   your shoes le sue scarpe
   (*singular, familiar*)
   your book il tuo libro
   your shirt la tua camicia
   your shoes le tue scarpe
yours: is this yours? è suo?
   (*singular, familiar*) è tuo?
youth hostel
   l'ostello della gioventù

zip la chiusura lampo
zoo lo zoo